THE
BRITISH ACADEMY
1949–1968

THE
BRITISH ACADEMY
1949-1968

BY

MORTIMER WHEELER

LONDON
PUBLISHED FOR THE BRITISH ACADEMY
BY THE OXFORD UNIVERSITY PRESS
1970

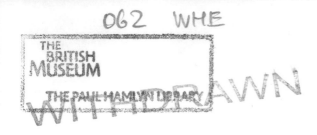
© THE BRITISH ACADEMY 1970

SBN 19 725921 9

PRINTED IN GREAT BRITAIN
AT THE UNIVERSITY PRESS, OXFORD
BY VIVIAN RIDLER
PRINTER TO THE UNIVERSITY

PREFACE

ON my retirement from the Secretaryship of the British Academy at the end of 1968, its Council invited me to record the Academy's Works and Days during the twenty years which had elapsed since my assumption of the office some time in 1949. In so doing it was following its own precedent. In 1949 it had asked my predecessor, Sir Frederic Kenyon, to record the first fifty years of the Academy's existence, a task which he was then, as the last survivor of the first generation of Fellows, uniquely qualified to do. His little book, published in 1952, preserves the main facts in worthy if summary fashion and, save for brief and necessary amplifications in my introductory chapter, is assumed in the following pages.

Kenyon suffered—or enjoyed?—one circumstance which has not confronted his successor: there were no systematic Academy files prior to 1949, no encouragement to the resurrection of proceedings and personalities such as have facilitated and perhaps a little overweighted the present review. For the rest, I would feel moved to describe this new volume as a Personal History but that I can recall no history which, for good or ill, cannot be so described. From moment to moment the writer appears variously as 'I' or 'the Secretary' in the hope of diverting the reader's attention from the individual to the facts related. For these at least a mass of minute-books and correspondence is a guarantee of accuracy; and I am glad to acknowledge also the friendly intervention of the Academy's former Assistant Secretary, Miss D. W. Pearson, whose meticulous memory has been at my service, particularly in regard to the earlier phases of the story. But she must not be blamed for its telling.

MORTIMER WHEELER

1970

CONTENTS

CONTENTS

LIST OF ILLUSTRATIONS

I

INTRODUCTORY

As the only survivor of those concerned with the institution of the British Academy in 1901, Sir Frederic Kenyon, on retirement from the Secretaryship in 1949, was invited to write its history in the context of the forthcoming jubilee of its Royal Charter. The result, a slim but useful volume of 37 pages, was published in 1952 as *The British Academy: the First Fifty Years*, with a foreword by Sir Charles Webster, then President. The main facts of the foundation and early history are there assembled, but certain of them may be restated and amplified as an introduction to a record of the succeeding phase.

Briefly, the Academy owes its origin to an *ad hoc* meeting of European and American academies held at Wiesbaden in October 1899, where it was resolved to set up a permanent international Association of Scientific and Literary Academies throughout the world. In this new Association, whilst the Royal Society represented Great Britain in the section 'Natural Science', no existing institution was at that date deemed competent to represent the equivalent Humanities. Accordingly, with the sympathetic understanding of the Royal Society, the British Academy was established as an unincorporated society on 17 December 1901, for the purpose of promoting 'Historical, Philosophical and Philological Studies' and, again with the support of the Royal Society, petitioned His Majesty in Council for the grant of a Royal Charter. On 8 August 1902, the Royal Charter was granted on the eve of the Coronation of King Edward VII.

So far, so good. But the new Academy was as yet a thing of little substance. On paper it possessed a President (Lord Reay, who had taken a prominent part in the initial negotiations), an Honorary Secretary (Israel Gollancz), and forty-seven other members, with an envisaged maximum of a hundred all-told. It was subdivided into four Sections: I, History and Archaeology; II, Philology (Oriental, Biblical, Classical, Medieval, Modern); III, Philosophy (Logic, Psychology, Ethics, Metaphysics, etc.); and IV, Jurisprudence and Economics. It possessed neither premises nor executive staff nor funds other than its own subscriptions.

Its reception by the interested public was understandably a mixed one. In particular, misconception arose from uninformed comparisons with the 'Forty Immortals' of the French Academy, who were traditionally concerned with the preservation of linguistic purity and included creative writers. Thus Max Beerbohm proclaimed:

Dryasdustocracy can offend no one—except perhaps such gentlemen as are out of it and might as well have been in it. . . . An academy could do no harm to literature. But it were a chronic pleasure to them who care for the comedy of life. Accordingly the notion of it is dear to me.

The error implicit in this and other remarks of the kind was traversed by Bernard Shaw, if with the inevitable Shavian sniff.

Academies of Letters, like Orders of Merit and other hallmarks of eminent achievement, have no more to do with the current hard work of life than Chelsea Hospital has with national defence. In the nature of things you cannot make a man an Academician until his bolt is shot. For example, Dr. Murray is a member of the new Academy, not because he is going to edit a New English Dictionary, but because he has already done it, for which reason he will be the last man in the world to call for a Newer English Dictionary. . . . The people who vaguely expected that the Academy would include the leading writers of fiction simply do not know the technical meaning of the word Letters. But in any case Fiction is ably represented by the historians.

In the earlier part of that observation, Shaw put his finger upon a basic weakness of the Academy during its opening half-century: its tendency to content itself with achieved eminence, rather than to establish a working contact with rising scholars and new ideas. I trust that in the course of the present review it may be possible to show that in the third quarter-century of the Academy's existence this static mood has changed, hopefully if still inadequately.

Not that the earlier decades were entirely devoid of activity. The Academy's first Secretary, (Sir) Israel Gollancz, energetically collected endowments for periodical lectures, and these, as published in the annual Proceedings, represent a formidable body of research. Of other publications, the nine substantial volumes of *Social and Economic Records*, issued between 1914 and 1935 with the help of a Treasury grant of £400 a year for three years (not renewed), constituted an enterprise of outstanding value. In 1914 the Academy took an active interest in the foundation of the School of Oriental Studies, and after the First World War it helped to promote (however ineffectively) the foundation of the British School of Archaeology in Jerusalem, and joined in a number of other appropriate enterprises. But it had not yet begun to dominate the world of Humanism in any measure remotely comparable with the ancient Royal Society's established dominance of the world of Science. Its lack of Government support both caused and reflected a lack of sustained initiative. Five years after the First World War the Academy still had no quarters, no paid staff, and no Government grant.

The long drawn-out attempt to secure a modest Treasury subsidy was, in retrospect, a sorry commentary upon the methods and policies of another age. With little enough to show in the shape either of actual achievement or of forward planning, the Academy negotiators were content to rely for the most part upon top-level interchange based upon old acquaintance and abstract assurance. As early as 1903, the year following its Royal Charter, the Academy was submitting to The Lords Commissioners of His Majesty's Treasury a lengthy printed memorandum, concluding with the airy affirmation that 'in the interests of the nation as a whole, as well as in the interests of those who are occupied in promoting these branches of scientific study, the Treasury ought to recognize the British Academy as the correlative of the Royal Society, and to grant it a similar support. In this way the Government would give to England that ordered and balanced organization for the pursuit of all branches of science which is already possessed by all the leading nations of Europe'. A. J. Balfour was at the time Prime Minister, but the answer, given in 1904, was *No*.

Twenty years later, the situation remained unchanged save that A. J. Balfour (now the Earl of Balfour, K.G., O.M.) had meanwhile become President of the Academy. With the aid of his predecessor in the Presidency, Sir Frederic Kenyon, a fresh approach was made to the Lords Commissioners of the Treasury, this time for a specific grant-in-aid of £2,000 'in order that the Academy might be enabled to perform its functions under suitable conditions'. The official move was supplemented by personal correspondence between Balfour and the Chancellor of the Exchequer, Neville Chamberlain. After some polite hesitation, Chamberlain finally responded on 21 January 1924:

Replying on the eve of the General Election I said that at first sight it appeared to me that the present time was inopportune for sanctioning new commitments of this kind, but that I should like to have time to look more fully into the question before reaching a final decision. I am afraid that a fuller examination of the matter only confirms my first

impression. I see that you yourself in 1904 felt unable in the then existing financial circumstances to sanction a grant to the Academy, and
subsequent applications have been refused on the same grounds of
financial stringency. . . .

Answer, again *No*.

Then slowly things—some things—began to happen. The
Conservative government suffered electoral defeat, and Neville
Chamberlain's successor, Philip Snowden, was immediately approached through Lord Haldane, Fellow of the Academy. At the
end of February 1924, twenty-three years after its foundation, the
Academy received approval from a Labour Government for its
first annual grant: £2,000.

Three years later, in its twenty-sixth year, the Academy at long
last added for the first time a habitation to its name. Lord Balfour,
as President, received a letter from Winston Churchill, as Chancellor of the Exchequer, informing 'My dear Arthur' that 'in
recognition of the position of the Academy and its services to the
nation, the Government has decided to assign it free quarters in
Burlington House'. In fact it received a small portion of the
ground floor of no. 6 Burlington Gardens, a substantial, porticoed
and be-sculptured mansion built in mid-Victorian days as the home
of the University of London and now to be shared with the Civil
Service Commission. In 1928, on 24 July, a formidable luncheon-
party was thrown (no women present) at the Prince's Hotel,
Piccadilly, nominally to mark the opening of the new rooms of the
Academy, but, as events materialized, factually to celebrate the
almost coincidental 80th birthday of Lord Balfour, the Academy's
President. In those more ample days the press-coverage was extensive, and it is abundantly clear that, after initial formalities,
Balfour was the usurping hero of the occasion, with the Prince of
Wales as runner-up. 'Today', said the Prince, 'we are thinking
about Lord Balfour', and it is perhaps worth an idle moment to
glance back through the eyes of the older journalism at our hero's
progress on that day from the purlieus of Pall Mall to the remote
altitudes of Burlington Gardens and Piccadilly.

The great A. J.

left his house in Carlton-gardens, S.W., [on his way to the British
Academy] wearing a frock coat and a silk hat and, swinging a heavy
walking stick heartily, walked briskly towards Pall Mall. With a cheery
wave of his stick to oncoming traffic, a happy little wave of warning,
Lord Balfour crossed busy Pall Mall and gained the opposite pavement
with a little leap. He was quite the most nimbly stepping man in St.
James's-square as, with his stick describing an occasional flashing

The Times photograph

1. At the opening of the Academy's quarters in Burlington Gardens, 24 July 1928. Left to right: Dr. J. W. Mackail, Sir Frederic Kenyon, Sir Charles Wakefield, Arnold Mitchell (architect), the Archbishop of Canterbury, the Lord Mayor of London, Lord Balfour (President), H. A. L. Fisher, and Sir Israel Gollancz (Secretary).

circle, he walked through York-street to Piccadilly, which he crossed after 20 seconds of adroit manoeuvring. His progress from Pall Mall to Piccadilly took considerably less time than that of Mr. Winston Churchill, who went to the same luncheon by motor-car . . .[1]

The luncheon was manifestly an agreeable and highly distinguished affair, with an atmosphere which the Prince described (with undisguised relief) as 'not oppressively academic'.

But behind this portentous scene occurred simultaneously an unsung academic event of some long-term significance. For the first time in its history the Academy acquired a Staff. True it was of minimal size, and its salary was less than minimal. Miss D. W. Pearson (now O.B.E.) had been a pupil of Gollancz's and had, at his instance, been helping the Foreign Office in its gigantic task of restoring the British section of the Imperial University Library of Tokyo, which had been utterly destroyed by earthquake in 1923. Now, in 1928, Gollancz brought her into the newly-housed Academy as its first Assistant Secretary, on a half-time basis. Two years later she assumed full-time duty in this solitary post; and until 1949 she remained the total paid staff of the Academy— forty-eight years after its foundation! More of this anon.

Came the World War of 1939. In 1940 the Treasury suspended its Academy grant, but a year later yielded to protest to the extent of restoring an annual subsidy of £1,000. This continued until 1946–7, when it was increased to £2,500—of course an utterly unviable sum under post-war conditions but at least a token gesture. It could, however, no longer be concealed that the Academy had reached its nadir and was nigh to death. The persistent distribution of obituaries of its Fellows throughout these years did little for the morale of the survivors; I recall that in all sorts of irrelevant corners of the world, from the deserts of Africa to the hills of Simla, those slim gravestones reminded me intermittently that, if the Academy no longer lived, at least it died with grace and honour. Let there be no misunderstanding in this remark. Collectively the Academy's obituaries constitute a primary and invaluable contribution to the history of British scholarship. But, save for endowed lectures, practically all other publication had ceased. When I came back to England for a few months in 1948 after several years overseas, the Academy meant almost nothing to me and, as I gathered from contemporary Fellows, very little to anyone else.

Here I may perhaps be allowed briefly to put myself into the picture. I had nominally been a Fellow since 1941, when a friend

[1] *Daily Mail*, 25 July 1928.

had quite irregularly told me in confidence that he and others
were putting me up for election. I am afraid that at the time
I had not been deeply moved by the news, though I was mildly
interested in what my communicative friend then proceeded to
say. I should explain that, like so many others in 1940 and there-
abouts, I happened to be dressed up as some sort of soldier. My
friend regarded the uniform with ill-concealed disapproval. 'Of
course', he said, 'we're not mentioning your rank. I don't think
they'd accept you as a scholar if they knew you were a colonel.'
And now, in 1948, one began to wonder in reverse, whether 'they'
were themselves in any valid sense worthy of acceptance.

This was in fact no new source of doubt and wonderment. On
28 April 1932, the first woman elected to the Academy, the
formidable Beatrice Webb, had recorded her first impressions of
the Fellowship after the Sectional meetings of that year. She described it as 'a funny little body of elderly and aged men—the aged
predominating', and she observed that 'the little crowd gave a
lifeless and derelict impression—very Oxford donnish and con-
ventional in culture and tone'. The most important business of
the Academy was 'canvassing for rival candidates to fill vacancies
up to the statutory limit'.[1] Comments of this sort were already
growing in force, when in 1949 (let it be said, not unprompted)
the President remarked in his annual address that he had 'previously referred to unfavourable criticisms passed upon the Academy, both within and without our Fellowship . . . The Academy
is not fulfilling as fully as it should the functions which it exists to
perform, and it does not enjoy that reputation or that place in the
national life which such a body might rightly claim.' He continued: 'our shortcomings may be attributed in large measure to
financial reasons. The effects of these are various. Our premises
are inconvenient and quite unworthy of such an institution. We
need a larger clerical staff. The sum available for publications is
inadequate . . . We have no library, nor even accommodation for
such books as are from time to time presented to us. We have no
room in which Fellows can conveniently meet . . .' And so on.

But, alas, the enumeration of shortcomings was not matched by
any commensurate plan of achievement, with priorities, speci-
fications, and costs. No effort was made to interest our masters
at the Treasury personally in our plight and potentiality. If the
Academy's 'shortcomings' could be attributed 'in large measure
to financial reasons', it would have been scarcely less true to

[1] Published in *Beatrice Webb's Diaries 1924–1932* (ed. Margaret Cole,
London, 1956), and cited in the Academy's Presidential Address 1956.

G.L.C. Photograph Library

2. Number 6, Burlington Gardens, designed in 1866–7 by Sir James Pennethorne as architect of the Office of Works to house London University. It was opened by Queen Victoria in 1870, and remained in the occupation of the University until 1900. Thereafter it was taken over by the Civil Service Commission, but from 1928 to 1968 a few rooms were placed at the disposal of the British Academy.

The façade is adorned with statues of illustrious worthies by J. S. Westmacott and other leading sculptors of the day, but Shakespeare, whose genius was regarded as 'independent of academic influence', was placed inside on the staircase.

The building is now (1969) on loan to the British Museum for the temporary housing of its Ethnographic Collections.

ascribe financial duress to the Academy's own manifest short-comings. In effect, the Academy was at a standstill. It had lost, if it had ever really acquired, urgent contact with contemporary need and circumstance, and a condition of complacency had supervened. Let the evidence come from its own mouth. In his *History of the First Fifty Years* of the Academy already referred to, Sir Frederic Kenyon was content to proclaim as late as 1949 that 'the Secretary must be able to be in town at least two or three days in each week' (!). And on the same page he was able, with un-conscious but pathetic irony, to boast that 'the Academy had now settled into its stride'. . . . It is only fair for me to recall hastily, as an old admirer of Sir Frederic, that he was by this time a very elderly gentleman and that in the early years of the Academy he had been one of its most assiduous champions.

Now, in 1949, it was, as nearly as might be, without effective leader. But happily not quite. In the ranks of the Council there was one member who saw more clearly than his colleagues: an honest, sociable, fearless, scholarly, internationally-minded son of Lancashire, the historian Charles Webster. That name should be written large in the annals of the Academy.

Exactly what happened I cannot record at first hand; I was not at that time a member of the Council and had indeed been an absentee-Fellow overseas since my election. But reliable report had it that at a meeting of the Council early in 1949 there had been a Palace Revolution. Sir Charles, unable to contain his im-patience, had demanded uninhibitedly a change in the Academy's administration, and Kenyon with characteristic coolness and courtesy had taken the point. He expressed his intention to resign the Secretaryship forthwith and to look round for a successor.

His task was not easy. The post was an honorary one (with a trivial expense-allowance) and, although allegedly part-time, was at the lowest estimate not devoid of some responsibility. In the *History* already quoted, Kenyon observes that 'the field of choice was small'. In this quandary, he was reduced to turning to me. We had known each other between the Wars, and in 1948 I had returned from the East to take up a part-time chair which my friends had discovered for me in the University of London. I suppose that the cap appeared to fit nearly enough. At any rate, the Council took the risk.

In 1949 I attended my first Council meeting, and, looking round the table, had no difficulty in seeing what was wrong.

II

SENIORES PRIORES

To recapitulate. In 1949 the Academy was in the forty-eighth year of its nominal existence. Its restricted quarters in Burlington Gardens were perhaps just adequate for a staff which comprised a very part-time Honorary Secretary in his eighty-seventh year, with one ill-paid Assistant Secretary as a maid-of-all-work. Apart from endowments of dwindling financial value for nine lectures—as already emphasized, an important primary asset due almost entirely to Israel Gollancz—its income consisted of an annual grant of £2,500 from H.M. Treasury. Half of the Council was in or beyond its seventies, and only mortality could bar indefinite re-election. The President was a charming, distinguished, and highly specialized scholar who had spent his life in a museum and had little practical comprehension either of forward broad-scale planning or of the competitive world of Whitehall. For an institution which had been the designated humanistic counterpart of the Royal Society, all this sounds impossible, but alas it was true.

I remember going for the first time a trifle timidly into the Academy's office and asking the Assistant Secretary for copies of correspondence. There were practically none; there were no systematic files whatsoever. My predecessor had dealt with his letters in good Victorian fashion, in other words, *propria manu*; the routine of stenography was since his time. Save when a meagre minute, or a chance-memory, or some subsequent interchange came to the rescue, the Academy's affairs were wrapped in mystery. I sat down at my table and sent out an S.O.S.

One of my signals reached Miss Margerie Taylor, an old and redoubtable friend of mine who occupied a cavern in the Ashmolean at Oxford. Her reply came back instantly and helpfully. She had an excellent part-time secretary who also 'did' for Sir Alan Gardiner, the Egyptologist, but might find two or three days a week for me, provided that I didn't steal her. I stole her, and thereafter fought with her for twenty years. For the pretty constant development of the Academy during that time she is by no means entirely guiltless. Her name is Molly Myers. As the Academy's income rose through the years, she accumulated round her a kaleidoscope of young and industrious girls. I had nearly echoed the flamboyant words of my predecessor, 'the Academy had now settled into its stride', but of course as yet it had scarcely begun. We were still tabulating some of our more obvious defects, a selection of which, as we have seen, was incorporated in that year's Presidential Address.

Time came (1950) for a change of President. I was still a new boy at the Academy, and conferred privately with my oldest friend, Sir Alfred Clapham, who was a member of the Council. I put to him the name of Sir Charles Webster, leader of what I have called the Palace Revolution, on the double or alternative plea that Webster was plainly a man of courage and initiative, and/or that he would be something of a nuisance otherwise than in the presidential chair; to which he was duly and very properly elected. As these words make manifest, at the time I did not yet know Webster personally. Subsequently and very quickly we became the closest of friends. Day-by-day, after lunch, we got together beside one of the gaunt fire-places of the Athenaeum's drawing-room and settled the affairs of the world with special reference to the Academy. We found that we shared revolutionary ideas and in argument we hatched dreadful plots.

This procedure, thus stated, sounds (I am told) highly conspiratorial and undemocratic, and in a limited sense it was. But in the circumstances it was right. As will be shown, at a critical moment in the Academy's history it worked, and was quite certainly the only workable method. At the time, the primary weakness of the Academy lay in the composition and outlook of its governing body, which was therefore in the worst possible condition itself to initiate its own reform. Strong and diplomatic leadership, carefully planned, was the prerequisite of successful innovation, always of course subject to ultimate democratic controls.

We began, then, by tackling the very obvious age-problem within our ranks, and we did so from two main angles. First, there was the regrettable fact that, by some obscure quirk of providence, Fellowship of the Academy appeared to involve a guarantee of preternatural longevity. Within our then-maximum membership of 175, the expectation of age was certainly a high one; incredibly, over twenty per cent of the Fellows were more than seventy-five years of age, with the corollary that vacancies for younger generations of scholars were unwholesomely restricted. Our annual intake of new Ordinary Fellows, covering ten Sections, rarely exceeded eight. At the same time, the academic world around us was already showing evidence of expansion.

Some sort of blood-transfusion was unmistakably needed if the Academy was to remain a useful working part of it.

Secondly, as I have noted above, elderly Fellows, often inadequately employed in retirement, tended to dominate our Council and committees (if any) and, once elected to them, to regard removal as a gratuitous indelicacy. The proper circulation of responsibility amongst the Fellowship at large had become an invidious issue to the point of impossibility.

The remedy for this second ill was not difficult. There were many precedents for limiting membership of the Council at any one stretch to a maximum term of years, and an amendment to the Academy's bye-laws in this sense was approved by the Council and Annual General Meeting in 1951 and by the Privy Council in 1952. Thenceforth continuous membership of the Council was limited to three years.

So far so good. Fresh faces, or old ones resurrected after seemly interval, could now be expected periodically at our governing board. But the basic problem of dominant antiquity in the Fellowship at large was less straightforward, if only because our faithful and numerous ancients would not unnaturally combine to resist the loss or reduction of their accustomed kingdom. The Athenaeum fire-place worked hard upon this problem for an appreciable time.

The outcome was that we (the President and the Secretary) decided upon two measures, both of which would require careful handling in transit. The first was essentially a short-term device: to enlarge the Fellowship, and therefore its immediate intake, in accordance with the trend and need of the times. There would of course be an inevitable outcry of 'inflation', 'dilution', 'a lowering of standards', and so forth; but we calculated that a modest increase from the then-maximum of 175 Fellows to one of 200 might be swallowed (as proved to be the case) without an excess of emotion. And this we had good reason to avoid, for a mild medicinal draft of this nature was no solution to the long-term problem. It would in ultimate effect do little more than enlarge the reservoir of elderly retireds. The permanent removal of the incubus of old age demanded some far more drastic and contentious remedy. It demanded, not medicine, but surgery. It meant nothing less than the removal of the more elderly Fellows from direct participation in the ultimate government of the Academy.

This was not indeed a new problem. As long ago as 1924, J. W. Mackail in his Presidential Address had drawn attention to 'the tendency in all Academies and Institutes—as it is perhaps in

other spheres also—to become encumbered with Elder Statesmen', and echoed a plea for more youthfulness and energy: 'a
student should be able to look forward to recognition while his
energies are still unexhausted . . . In the last three years the
average age of the twenty-nine Fellows elected was over sixty . . .
Seven were in their seventies.' He reminded his audience that 'in
the Royal Academy of Arts there is a class of Senior Academicians—there are twelve of them at present—who are outside of
the traditional forty Academicians prescribed in the Instrument
of 1768'. But the British Academy was not amused, and Mackail's
very sensible hint passed into limbo.

Now in 1951, without in fact back-reference to Mackail, the
problem presented itself with a fresh acuteness to the President
and the Secretary, confronted by this passive challenge of established seniority. Renewed and perhaps extravagant opposition to
reform could be foreseen, but Webster was a master of diplomacy
with international experience. He realized from the outset that
haste would be fatal to the revolutionary scheme which had now
been matured in our minds after no little private argument and
enquiry in the early months of the year. It was clear that to follow
the normal procedure of consulting the Council in this matter
beforehand was to court certain failure, since the Council was,
as we have seen, the stronghold of entrenched age and privilege.
Accordingly, in his first Presidential Address, delivered in July
of that year, Webster went straight to the general Fellowship
and took it into his confidence. He was right. The actuality
or suspicion of preliminary back-stairs intrigue, which could
only have inflamed a situation capable of generating a considerable heat, was in large measure obviated or at least diffused and
diminished.

The relevant words in the 1951 Presidential Address are
these:

We all rejoice, I think, that men, including scholars, live longer than
they used to do and not only longer but more vigorously in their old
age. Some of our most active scholars have long passed three-score years
and ten. But this has meant that, in a limited society such as ours,
members are often not elected until an age when other responsibilities
make it difficult for them to co-operate to the full in the activities of the
Academy. My own view, made after much reflection, and after discussing the question with members of European academies, is that the time
has come to make a category of senior members, who, while retaining
all their rights and privileges, will not be expected to take the same part
in our administrative activities. They should also, in my opinion, no

longer have to pay any subscription. If this course be adopted we will be able to elect a larger number of members at a younger age without injury to the standards of our scholarship or the finances of the Academy. I intend in the coming year to lay this proposal before the Council, and, if they adopt it, to bring it before you at our next Annual General Meeting. I state this intention now so that it may receive your earnest consideration and that you may, if you wish to do so, either in meetings of the Sections or as individuals, make your views known to the Council before they themselves take a decision upon it.

That was surely an eminently balanced and restrained pronouncement. But the sequel was long and on occasion stormy. The Old Guard was not going down without a fight. The main proposals, as submitted in due course to the Council and Sections of the Academy were these:

(a) That, with the approval of the Privy Council, Fellows on reaching the age of 75 shall be regarded as supernumerary to the authorized establishment of the Academy.

(b) That in future, therefore, no-one over the age of 74 will be admitted to Ordinary Fellowship. (Corresponding and Honorary Fellowship were not affected.)

(c) That Fellows on reaching the age of 75 shall retain their Fellowship of the Academy without further payment.

(d) That such Fellows shall continue to receive the publications of the Academy on the same terms as Ordinary Fellows.

(e) That such Fellows shall retain the right of full participation in Sectional and General Meetings, but shall not be eligible for membership of the Council.

The sting was of course in the tail. For the rest there was little to which objection could be sustained. But the sting pierced to the heart of the problem, and when the scheme reached the Sections, as it did during the following months, the general reaction can only be described as actively defensive. Of eight voting Sections, four were strongly or even unanimously against the proposal and only two were wholly for it. Webster and I held a council of war and decided that a good deal more groundwork would have to be done before the project could be put with assurance to an Annual General Meeting. In his Presidential Address for 1952, Webster therefore merely remarked that 'the response [to the proposal for the creation of a category of Senior Fellows] has shown that the Academy is not yet willing to follow this course. The fact that under our new bye-laws we can extend our membership to two hundred makes the problem less urgent.'

But the battle was not over. At the fire-place it was increasingly obvious to us that the exclusion of antiquated Fellows from the Council was more than ever essential to the progress and well-being of the Academy. Analysis showed quite easily that opposition to reform came almost exclusively from or through obstructive elders and was prompted by the human instinct for self-preservation rather than by rational argument. Gradually, in the course of more or less casual interchanges, better sense prevailed; and when, in April 1953, the scheme was again formally canvassed, only two out of the eleven Sections voting remained in opposition. At last the battle was won, save for a little ultimate shouting. Looking down upon the gathering at the Annual General Meeting in July of that year, the platform could not help observing the presence of an unusual number of the more elderly Fellows, clearly in battle-trim. Nevertheless, when the proposal for the creation of a category of Senior Fellows came up for discussion, an amendment was defeated and the proposition was carried 'by a large majority'. In due course the new rules were ratified by the Privy Council, and it was felt by some of us that in an appreciable measure the Academy had achieved a fresh and much-needed lease of life.

This chapter has dealt mainly with Old Age in the Academy after the Second World War, and there can be no doubt that in 1950 we were right in regarding this as our primary domestic problem. It is only fair to add as a postscript, however, that the ill was not restricted to the British Academy. For five or six years the younger generations of much of the civilized world had been ponded back in war-time back-waters whilst at the same time their elders, cosseted by modern science and stimulated by continuing employment, retained at least a specious semblance of middle-aged normality, unaware of the approaching shadows. This was brought home to me when, in 1951, I joined Charles Webster and Roger Mynors in their annual visit to Brussels as representatives of the Academy at the Union Académique Internationale. It may be recalled that the meeting of European and American academies at Wiesbaden in 1899, at which the first seed of the British Academy was sown (p. 1), had drawn up a scheme for the organization of an International Association of the principal Scientific and Literary Academies of the World. This perished in the First World War but, on French initiative, was replaced in 1919 by two new bodies: an Association of Academies of Natural Science and a Union Académique Internationale (the U.A.I.) to deal with the equivalent humanities. On the latter body, the Academy represented the United Kingdom, and to it Webster, with his international enthusiasms, was devotedly attached. His lovable and shamelessly Churchillian French echoed gaily down the corridors, and in due course he, like Mynors after him, became President of the assembly.

Over the years the U.A.I. had accumulated a wide range of highly respectable projects, extending from medieval philosophy to classical cartography. Inevitably, these projects were, by 1950, in a very varying condition: a few of them, such as the Monuments of Byzantine Music and the Medieval Latin Dictionary, were perceptibly alive, whilst others were patently in a state of lapse or collapse. A glance round the assembled scholars at Brussels again revealed the basic cause. Many of them were of advanced age—Perpetual Secretaries and the like—and, save for rare exceptions such as Roger Mynors, the faces of younger scholars who should have been there were notably absent. For a week this elderly gathering pottered about from committee-room to committee-room, half-doing with a somewhat pretentious formality tasks which could well have justified three organized days. Midway through the week I freely confess that, in the classic words, my patience was exhausted.

In the aeroplane on the way back, I scribbled a lengthy note and passed it to Charles Webster in front of me. As he read it I could see that to him it was painfully near to sacrilege, and for a moment our new friendship was in peril. But not for long. Webster's liberality was a constant model to me, from which, no doubt, I have failed to profit. We argued a while, and ultimately agreed that something might and should be done to the U.A.I. After all, the first motive for the Academy's foundation in 1901 had been the provision of national representation of the humanities at the organic predecessor of this international body, and its continuing efficiency remained—and remains—our professional concern. No doubt in part through Webster's diplomatic intervention, a number of satisfactory changes were shortly introduced. In particular, the annual session was reduced from six to four days, and a number of projects were usefully redistributed. I have no recent first-hand knowledge of the U.A.I.'s proceedings, but there are abundant signs that time and a new generation of scholars have wrought many of the changes which in the middle of the century were very evidently overdue.

During these tedious but urgent processes of rejuvenation both at home and abroad, the proper functions of the Academy as an instrument of research had not been forgotten. But in a real sense we had first to fight for recognition, particularly in the purlieus of Whitehall, where we were still barely a name. (A knighthood, for example, bestowed upon the Secretary in 1952 had nothing to do with the Academy which, as Webster told me, had not even been consulted.) To Whitehall we must now turn.

III

BRITISH SCHOOLS AND INSTITUTES OVERSEAS

As has been related, from time to time since 1903 the Academy had petitioned the government for financial aid, in kind if not in degree comparable with the subventions long provided for its elder counterpart, the Royal Society. The approaches had invariably been through the medium of formal correspondence at top level, either with ministers of the Crown or with very senior civil servants. In those circumstances, it followed that the attack had been conducted without reserves, and the 'enemy' had been fully apprised from the outset of the aims, resources, and weaknesses of the attacker. Successful counter-attack in this war-game was thus rendered all too easy and tempting, as episode after episode had shown. The Neville Chamberlain fiasco (p. 3) had been merely one of many instances of the futility of this archaic procedure.

In 1950 a fresh mind, experienced in a more modern tradition, had no hesitation in adopting entirely different tactics. It so happened that since 1924 the new Secretary had been concerned annually (save when soldiering) in the extraction of funds either from the Whitehall Treasury or from its close counterpart in New Delhi for cultural projects of a variety of kinds. And he had found one method infallible; that was, to *interest* the middle or upper-middle grades of the Treasury personally in the business of the moment, to *consult* the officer concerned face to face (of course along premeditated lines), to involve him as one's partner, and, above all, *never to exaggerate* demands. Sweet reasonableness and complete openness were the key-notes of the whole exchange. Nor was this a mere exercise of elementary cunning. Time and again, both in London and in Delhi, these officers have become my very good friends, and in argument we have learned much, and happily, from one another. Very rarely, and then always in consultation with them, has it been necessary or helpful to go over their heads —twice or thrice only, I think, in my twenty years at the Academy. Written communications were normally restricted to the confirmation or recording of verbal agreements. Amicable discussion of ways and means, followed by the equally amicable discussion of luncheon-claret, is in my experience both a more agreeable and a more sensibly productive catalyst than a ream of foolscap.

Accordingly, in 1949–50 one of my first tasks was to discover some good reason for making personal contact with our Treasury masters and to observe at close range their temper and temperament. It was unnecessary to look very far. For five years—since the end of the Second World War—there had been uncertainty and discussion between the Government (particularly the Foreign Office), the British Museum, the Academy, and others as to the best method of estimating and paying the annual Treasury contribution which wholly or largely sustained those rather miscellaneous institutions, our Research Schools and Institutes abroad. For example, in November 1946 the Director of the British Museum wrote a trifle plaintively to Kenyon, as Secretary of the Academy, to the effect that the situation was then as follows: the British School at Rome would approach the Treasury direct; the British School at Athens had sent its application to him (the Director); the British School at Jerusalem had applied through the British Academy; from the British School in Iraq no information had been received; the Egypt Exploration Society, which was then seeking to establish a School at Cairo, had applied both to the Foreign Office and to the British Academy; and the (proposed) Anglo-Turkish Institute in Ankara had also applied to the Academy. The unhappy Treasury, with no inside knowledge of any of these institutions, actual or in contemplation, was at a loss, and confusion reigned: the inevitable inheritance of the long-standing lack of sensible co-ordination between the British Schools abroad, the Academy, and the Treasury.

And yet as far back as 1931, H. A. L. Fisher as President of the Academy had urged that the dispensation of Government funds to archaeological work

should be undertaken under the direction of the British Academy. At present the Treasury made a grant to the British Academy and separate grants to the Schools of Athens and Rome. The Treasury did not seem to be a body ideally well-fitted to assess the comparative claims of various learned enterprises such as those connected with the British Schools of Athens and Rome. It would seem natural that the State should turn to the Academy for advice on the administration of any grants which it might be disposed to make to learned purposes in the field of the humanities (*The Times*, 16 July 1931).

This exhortation fell on deaf ears. True, in some sense the Academy was then or later privileged to supply the Treasury with lists of the funds required by the British Schools and other archaeological projects overseas. It is evident, however, that the Treasury retained a close and direct control over the resultant grants and dispensed them without close consultation. For example, at the February Council Meeting of 1947 it is recorded that a letter was read from Sir Thomas Barlow

stating that, in reply to the applications of the various Schools of Archaeology forwarded by the Academy, the Treasury had decided to include in the Estimates for 1947–48 grants of £3,000 each to the British Schools at Rome, Athens, and in Iraq, and the Egypt Exploration Society, and £5,000 for the proposed new Anglo-Turkish Institute at Ankara. They did not consider it advisable to make a grant to the British School at Jerusalem in view of the unsettled state of Palestine, and also there were doubts whether the School performed functions which could not equally well be carried out by the Palestine Department of Antiquities.

The latent ignorance in that ex-cathedra reply must have been manifest to the recipient Academy but there is no indication that any protest—certainly any effective protest—was made to Their Lordships. In February 1949 a similarly categorical letter was received, again without resistance. It was clear, at any rate to a newcomer, that the time had come for the Academy to assert its specialized authority in these matters.

But before recording the sequel it may be useful to survey very briefly the history of these rather remarkable institutions of ours overseas. Most of them were specifically schools of archaeology and history, but the best of them had interpreted this function in a liberal spirit, and had in effect become cultural embassies of high non-political value. In 1950 there were five of them: at Athens, Rome, Jerusalem, in Iraq, and now at Ankara (mentioned above in its formative stage). To these could be added the Egypt Exploration Society although it had no permanent headquarters in Egypt. (The scheme to establish one in Cairo after the War came to nothing.) Years later, two new Institutes were added, in East Africa and Iran; of these something will be said later (pp. 65 ff., 75 ff.).

The oldest of these establishments is the British School of Archaeology at Athens, founded in 1885 on the initiative of the then Prince of Wales, Mr. Gladstone, and other prominent statesmen, reflecting the traditional enthusiasms which were at the time being rekindled by Schliemann's exploits at Troy and Mycenae. For its first ten years the new School, in the fashion of the time, managed to subsist somewhat sparingly upon private donations.

In 1895, difficulties loomed, and urgent approach by the British Museum, the Royal Society, and other bodies to H.M. Treasury produced an annual government grant of £500. Today (1969) that grant is £27,000 and is by no means excessive.

Thereafter, in 1901, the British School at Rome was established as an institute of archaeology, history, and letters, and, with the help of the Commissioners of the 1851 Exhibition, was enlarged after the International Exhibition held in Rome in 1911 to make provision for students of Architecture and the Fine Arts. In 1906 it had received its first Treasury grant of £500, and this stands today at £30,000.

The British School of Archaeology in Jerusalem was founded in 1919 as the first British School of the kind outside Europe. For a long time, however, it lacked both the funds and the direction needed to give it status as an effective training or research centre, and for some years before 1949 it had become an inoperative lodger in the well-financed American School in the Jordanian sector of the city, with no income at all from the British government. In the current year, from this source it has received £19,500.

The British School of Archaeology in Iraq was opened in 1932 as a memorial to the life and work of Gertrude Bell, and in 1947 it received a grant of £3,000 as a needed addition to its own private funds. Today its government subvention is £21,000.

The British Institute of Archaeology at Ankara was inaugurated in 1948 on wide and influential representation to H.M. Treasury and with promptings from the Foreign Office. It is entirely dependent upon Government grants which in the present year amount to £23,000.

The Egypt Exploration Society embodied the earlier Egyptian Exploration Fund in 1919, its purpose being to obtain and publish information respecting ancient and less ancient Egypt by literary or archaeological enquiry. It operates from the U.K. with the aid of seasonal camps in Egypt. For many years the Society was able to subsist on private donations, but in the changing conditions of the post-war years it received a grant of £3,000 from H.M. Treasury through the Academy in 1947, and this grant has now risen to £10,000. It also administered special grants amounting to £43,000 secured by the Academy from the Treasury as a contribution to an international campaign of archaeological salvage in the Nubian reaches of the Nile at the time of the building of the Aswan High Dam between 1960 and 1964, and the consequent flooding of 300 miles of the Nile valley.

It was very evident in 1950 that some measure of tidying up in the administration of these partially similar but also partially disparate institutions, particularly *vis-à-vis* the Treasury and, indeed, in respect of their general financial viability, had become inevitable and indeed urgent. At the same time, it was important for their well-being that nothing should be done to conflict with or seem to conflict with their individual independence and their quite distinctive personalities. Their varied origins and environments, the diverse historical, archaeological and other potentialities of the regions in which they were situate, the propinquity or absence of other international missions of the kind, even the simple factor of remoteness from London, all combined with the characters and qualities of successive directors to induce differences in policy and achievement which on the whole could not be regarded otherwise than as an academic asset. When, therefore, Webster and I went down to the Treasury to discuss the problem of a measure of centralization, we did not go as colonists in search of an empire but as explorers on a mission of discovery: a mission to find a solution for an administrative tangle which had by now become a notorious embarrassment in an appreciable sector of our academic world. More exactly, we went to confer with a Third Secretary, and a happy fate directed us to (Sir) Edward Playfair.

The ensuing conversation ranged, as we intended that it should, not merely over the question of the Schools, but over the whole extent of the Academy's financial future as at that time we visualized it. The immediate problem was settled at once: in surprisingly brief argument the Treasury affirmed that it would be delighted and relieved if the Academy would act in first instance as its authoritative agents in the submission of all the annual School budgets to Their Lordships. When we turned from principle to detail, there was one momentary hitch. The School in Jerusalem, as already indicated, had not received a Treasury grant for many years. Indeed, to all appearances it had ceased to exist; at best, it had been absorbed into the American School. To renew a lapsed grant under the conditions of post-war economy would be to re-found the School, and the establishment in effect of a new School could not at present be contemplated. I felt, however, that Playfair was reluctant in this verdict, and was trying hard to pull his punches. It was worth another try. 'In that case, I take it that H.M. Government is prepared to hand over our traditional cultural charge, Jerusalem, unreservedly to the Americans? That of course is what this negative decision amounts

3. Sir Charles Webster (President 1950–1954).

to.' Playfair thought a moment and then said, I think relievedly, 'Well, look here, suppose we give you £1,000 for Jerusalem.' The door was ajar! The School, potential centre of vital research, was shortly re-opened in its own quarters.

But the episode underlined the new needs of a changing world. No research school of this kind could, in 1952, be run literally on £1,000 or £2,000 a year. The fact that the Jerusalem institution did re-open and forthwith proceeded to carry out on a large scale exploratory work now of international fame, first at Jericho and later at Jerusalem itself, was essentially due, not to the modest generosity of H.M. Treasury, but to the fortunate availability of a scholar of first-class quality, fortified by a small but useful domestic bank-balance and other accessible outside resources. In days gone by Dr. Kathleen Kenyon (now Principal of St. Hugh's at Oxford) had already, under the British mandate, carried out archaeological work in the old Palestine; and now she was ready and eager to go back to the Near East and to devote some part of each year and of her own income first as honorary Director of the Jerusalem School and later as its Chairman. In all this she was in fact a survivor from a bygone age, when academic charity, as it might be called, came often enough to the rescue of academic indigence or parsimony; when the Director of any one of our Schools abroad could be both prepared and able to supplement a more or less nominal salary from his own pocket.

Those days of 'academic charity' were now drawing to an end, as private incomes dwindled. Skilled or semi-skilled amateurs were rapidly yielding place perforce to formally qualified professionals paid at more or less professional rates. To anticipate, a conference of our overseas Schools and Institutes, called by the Academy in 1964 to consider matters of staffing and status, agreed that in future the Directors of these institutions should, at least implicitly, be regarded as of professorial standing, with appropriate salary. This step had in fact long been taken by foreign schools of the kind, and only a characteristically lingering adherence to amateurism as opposed to professionalism in the insular British mind had delayed inevitable conformity.

In one way and another, Playfair had impressed us with the readiness of his Treasury to listen and to understand. In the years that followed we had no reason to vary that impression. The secular change of personnel in Whitehall brought no change to a continuously friendly and fructuous relationship. Amongst many Treasury names which could be recorded here with gratitude for sympathetic guidance, I court invidiousness for singling out one

—that of Richard Griffiths, sometime Under Secretary at the Treasury, now Deputy Secretary of the University Grants Committee, and my personal friend. Griffiths in some of our most crucial years piloted our little ship with skill and (in my recollection) uniform success through the variable inshore waters of Whitehall.

IV

PERIODICAL PUBLICATIONS

FROM 1950 onwards our consultations with our new partners at H.M. Treasury spread over an increasing range of interests and were reflected in a steady if still modest amplification of the Academy's annual budget. In 1949 the Government grant had been £2,500; in 1950 it was £5,000; in 1955 it was £41,950. These figures are now recorded not for the mere glorification of arithmetic but as the simplest token of the fact that we were winning the confidence of our masters in Whitehall and that a few at least of the Academy's proper objectives were a little nearer to attainment. Our growing budget could be seen to imply a steady growth of responsibility, and added tacitly to our weight and status in negotiation. The largest single advance was the consequence of the absorption of the overseas Schools into the Academy's estimates, as recorded in the last chapter. But this new addition to our functions brought with it no merely mechanical enlargement of our annual income. In the post-war years, these institutions were in a parlous state. One of them, as we have seen, had in effect ceased to exist. Another—and that the oldest of them—was discarding commitments and eating into capital almost to the extent of bankruptcy. One and all, they were in no sort of condition to yield a justifiable return in terms of training and output even for such meagre funds as were still available to them. They all needed a careful nursing back to health. Over the years the Academy has been able to help all of them to solvency or even to expansion. But it has been an arduous task and is not yet complete, if only because the unceasing struggle against monetary factors such as inflation and devaluation has been a constant hazard in the path of new achievement.

At the same time there were during the 'fifties several rival claimants upon the Academy's interest and ingenuity. Funds available to assist research, particularly amongst the younger scholars, who were rightly becoming increasingly importunate, were pitifully inadequate. For its own part, the Academy was not yet in a financial position to initiate any major project specifically its own. Not least, learned publications were everywhere in arrears. The Academy's own *Proceedings* had been largely suspended during the latter part of the War, and, although two volumes were now being printed each year, much of the material was liable to have become a trifle stale through long keeping. The periodicals of other learned bodies were in similar or worse case, many of them with very little prospect of catching up. The Academy helped here and there to the limit of its very inadequate resources. And then, when this notorious predicament showed every sign of further deterioration, help reached the Academy itself, together with the Royal Society which was in similar straits, from an unexpected quarter.

The good fairy was that far-seeing institution the Nuffield Foundation. In November 1953 both the Royal Society and the Academy received from Nuffield Lodge parallel enquiries: 'I am at present attempting to obtain some information for our Trustees on the current conditions of the learned journals and I am wondering if at any time recently you have had cause to make similar investigations of those journals concerned with the Humanities. I would be most grateful for an opportunity to talk over the whole problem with you. . . .' The information asked for was readily forthcoming under headings appropriate to the Academy, and the situation was revealed in all its starkness. In Classical studies the position of the important Societies had recently reached a critical stage, approaching bankruptcy. . . . The situation was 'extremely discouraging for scholars, particularly young scholars, who were forced either to wait for publication or to publish in journals where their studies were not easily seen'. Subscriptions had been advanced to the point of diminishing returns. In Oriental studies, at a time when Asian interests were occupying so important a place in world affairs, the institution best qualified to interpret Asian history and culture in the West was in a feeble condition, producing a meagre journal unworthy alike of the Society and of the vast region with which it dealt. In Philosophy, the publication of the Royal Institute was deeply and increasingly in debt, and other working-charges had been doubled. In Historical studies, several bodies of the highest value to scholarship could no longer subsist on the subscriptions of scholars alone. . . . In Archaeology the vast amount of salvage-excavation resulting from war-work and war-damage had alone built up a special body of research-material which had thrown an impossible burden upon the appropriate institutions. . . .

And so on, in similar vein. The bleak outlook had in fact already been stressed broadly in July of that same year 1953 by Webster in his Presidential Address. Now in one direction at least the tentative intervention of the Nuffield Foundation offered a ray of hope.

Conversations between the officers of the Nuffield Foundation (Leslie Farrer-Brown and J. E. Morpurgo) and the Secretaries of the Royal Society and the Academy (David Martin and myself) quickly gave a rational shape to the new situation. To facilitate discussion a notional figure of £8,000 a year (to be divided between the two Societies for a strictly limited period of five years) was mentioned as the extent of possible Nuffield assistance. Further, it was explained at the outset that at their last meeting the Trustees of the Foundation, while expressing a general wish to help the learned journals, had felt some misgivings as to whether their incursion in the field for such a short period might not have an effect opposite to its intentions, for some journals, they felt, might be lured into a sense of financial security while others, kept from the immediate risk of bankruptcy with Foundation money, would nevertheless be unable to prevent an eventual reckoning. The Trustees were, in addition, uncertain as to the effect, at the moment and after the end of the five-year period, that their grant might have on Government financial support.

These fears and hesitations were natural enough at the time, but it may be useful here, in the light of experience in this and comparable circumstances in later years, to declare their invalidity. Administered under clear-cut conditions, short-term aid has been proved to serve as a solid stimulus and precedent rather than as an *ignis fatuus*; whilst Government is often readier to follow up and support experienced self-help (i.e. the considered exploitation of private sources) than to provide wholly *de novo*. A further notable example of this, supplied by the Pilgrim Trust, will be cited on a later page. Meanwhile the Trustees of the Nuffield Foundation did not press their fears.

In these preliminary discussions it was agreed that the proposed grants should be administered through the normal channels of the two Societies, with a small unofficial joint-committee at executive level (Farrer-Brown, David Martin, and myself) to adjust details. Moreover it was agreed in principle that conditions appropriate to the individual grants should be imposed with professional advice from an unofficial panel of publishing advisers in receipt of fees provided separately by the Foundation. It may be recorded that the Academy's files include a typewritten *Report to the Nuffield Foundation on the Present State of Learned Journals* by (Sir) Robert Lusty—a lively and original memorandum but scarcely relevant to the present context. These and other procedures were approved by the Trustees of the Foundation on 29 June 1954. Thereafter for five years the Academy was able to award carefully considered grants, fortified by professional advice as to type, format, subscription-rates and the like, to a considerable number of 'primary' journals (twenty-five in the first year) dealing with 'primary' subjects. (The term 'primary' was never defined, but none of us had any disturbing doubt as to its intentions; it implied the organs of national bodies situated normally in London, Oxford, or Cambridge.) In one way and another it would be difficult to exaggerate the beneficent effect of this critically constructive and generous aid to the whole range of central learned periodicals. One by one they gradually emerged from the slough of despond into which a majority of them had drifted.

In June 1957 an annotated and analytical report on the administration of the grants awarded by the Academy from the Nuffield grant, together with comments by the grantees, was circulated by the Academy to its own Council and to the Nuffield Foundation. A further report covering 1958–9 was similarly distributed in 1959. During the five years of the grant, the allocations provided by the Foundation for the Academy were as follows:

1955–6	£4,500
1956–7	£4,500
1957–8	£4,250
1958–9	£3,750
1959–60	£3,750

The gradual reduction in the allocation fairly represented the diminishing needs of the periodicals concerned, as lee-way was made good, economies were effected, and circulations increased. It was agreed alike by the Foundation and by the Academy that the whole scheme had satisfactorily achieved some of its principal aims, though certain periodicals—particularly those of a highly specialized kind—would continue to require a measure of subvention. There was moreover the almost annual bogey of increasing printers' charges. The problem had in fact been mitigated at a critical moment, but not eliminated.

In 1960 the Nuffield grant came to its appointed end, and a brief word may be added as to the sequel. These annual subventions to selected periodicals had by now become a worthwhile and indeed necessary feature of the academic scene, and a sudden cessation of them was from several points of view highly undesirable. Accordingly, in his first year of Presidential office, Sir

Maurice Bowra looked about him for a successor-benefactor, and found it in All Souls College. As from Warden to Warden, on 22 March 1960, Mr. Sparrow wrote to Sir Maurice from All Souls as follows: '. . . This particular case seems so very deserving and the appeal came from a quarter which commended itself so strongly to the College generally that, after very thorough discussion, we felt able to return to it a favourable answer. . . . The College's resolution was to contribute up to £3,500 per annum for a period of three years. I hope you will feel that this is better than nothing.' Indeed it was, and at the end of the three years the burden thus generously sustained was passed on to a new Government research fund, of which more will be said later. The foundations planned under the Nuffield benefaction had been well and truly laid.

V

RESEARCH: (i) THE PILGRIM TRUST'S PILOT-SCHEME

To recapitulate again: the funds placed at the disposal of the Academy by the Nuffield Foundation (£20,750) and subsequently by All Souls College (£10,500) had served their immediate function of enabling selected journals to dispose of backlog, enlarge circulation, and carry out technical improvements under skilled advice. Apart from these material effects, the general encouragement given to the journals was a timely stimulus in many ways to authors and to editors. But all this might perhaps be described, though not ungratefully, as salvage rather than creation. Increasingly at this time our minds were troubled with the positive and expanding needs presented by the aspirations of a new generation of scholars inadequately provided under post-war conditions with the facilities and tools needed for sustained studentship; and specific examples of these needs had not only been brought to our notice but had received from us such limited response as was practicable. Happily, this anxiety was not confined to the professional circles of the Academy. On 11 November 1954, the Academy's Secretary received from Lord Kilmaine, Secretary of the Pilgrim Trust, a momentous letter from which extracts may be quoted:

Research in the Humanities and the Arts

For some time the Pilgrim Trustees have been investigating the question of whether there is a need to provide quite small grants ranging, say, from £50 to £200 to assist scholars in the field of the Humanities and the Arts to prosecute their research. The Trustees are not interested in the Sciences, since by and large industry, which derives direct benefit from scientific research, should be able to support it. The Humanities and the Arts, on the other hand, it has been suggested, are as it were 'starved' in this respect. The Trustees have felt that, if they could be convinced of the need, they might themselves establish a fund, placed for purposes of administration in the hands of some suitable body, from which grants might be allocated to deserving scholars (as distinct from immature students) in the field of the Humanities and the Arts.

The Pilgrim Trustees had thought that any fund which they might establish should be used for grants for the following purposes:

(1) Travel in connexion with the applicant's subject.
(2) The making or purchase of photographs or microfilms bearing on his subject.
(3) The provision of a 'sabbatical' period to enable a scholar to pursue a particular piece of work in freedom from financial anxiety.
(4) The provision of secretarial help for typing, etc., to enable a scholar to devote his whole attention to his main work.

The Trustees are aware that many scholars find difficulty in getting the results of their research work published, but they do not feel disposed to consider subsidizing publications because they feel that the applications would be legion. . . .

My Trustees instructed me to ask you two things—first, whether you and other officers of the British Academy can contribute from experience any opinion as to the existence of a need for grants. . . . And secondly, supposing that the Pilgrim Trustees were to place in the hands of the British Academy a sum of say £1,000 to £2,000 p.a. for an experimental period of three years, would the Academy be able to make effective use of it in helping individual scholars to carry to a conclusion work of high value to scholarship which otherwise could never be concluded or might not be concluded for a long time? . . .

At the end of the experimental period my Trustees would like to review all the cases which had been helped out of the fund in the light of a report from the administering body to see whether any case had been made out for the establishment of some such fund . . . on a permanent basis.

If you would like to talk to me . . .

That letter began nine years of the closest possible co-operation between the Academy and the Trust, through the media of letters, annual reports and, not least, highly agreeable and profitable luncheons. The Academy's President at the time of the approach was Sir George Clark, and he, Kilmaine, and the Academy's Secretary made a thoroughly sympathetic triumvirate. Looking back through our interchanges, I am particularly struck with Lord Kilmaine's judicious co-operativeness; preliminary problems were smoothly and promptly ironed out, and by 21 February 1955 Kilmaine was able to report (with an enclosed cheque) that the Pilgrim Trustees were 'entirely satisfied with the proposals made in your letter for publicizing and for administering the fund during the experimental period', and had accordingly voted a grant of £2,000 p.a. to the British Academy for the next three years.

In amplification, it may be recorded that the fund was distributed by the Academy's Council on the advice of a committee consisting of the Chairmen of the Academy's eleven Sections together with the Director of the British Museum and a representative of the Museums Association, sitting under the over-all chairmanship of the Academy's President. As to publicity, it was felt that the number and size of the grants which we should be able to make would scarcely be large enough to justify public advertisement or official notification to all the institutions in which possible recipients worked. Nor was it thought appropriate or economic to sift the very large number of good cases to enable us to test the problem on an adequate academic and geographical scale. For this purpose we corresponded with a limited number of selected individuals, including representatives of the art-gallery world, the major libraries and museums, and certain of the universities. In practice this somewhat rule-of-thumb method produced satisfactory results within the limited scope of the experiment.

At the end of the first and subsequent years, the Academy submitted to the Pilgrim Trustees an annotated list of awards (14 in the first year) together with interim reports from the beneficiaries. On the first occasion the Trustees, in return, were pleased to express 'their great pleasure and praise at the way in which the Academy had administered this grant and at the range of subjects which the awards had covered. They considered that the money had been used for exactly the sort of purpose which they had had in mind. They would wish to ask you to continue the good work on the same lines'. As a hint of the range of approved subjects may be mentioned from the first list: 'Expenses in connection with a fresh survey of a part of the temple of Apollo at Bassae for the purpose of identifying the original positions of the reliefs now in the British Museum' [a task very successfully accomplished and now illustrated in the new Bassae room opened in 1969]; 'Research on coin collections in Spain'; 'For photostats and travel in connection with the preparation of a corpus of facsimiles of dated Hebrew MSS to be published in Denmark'; 'For a survey of Christian antiquities in Cyrenaica under the auspices of the British School at Rome'; 'For a 3-month visit to Spain in connection with work on the colonizing enterprises in North America of the Elizabethan explorers'; 'For photographs for work on the text of Seneca's *Epistulae Morales*'; 'For an expedition to Urfa and Taktek Mountains to study Syrian inscriptions'; 'For the preparation of a new edition of Jeremy Bentham's *Deontology or Science of Morality*'; 'For travel to Istanbul and Mount Athos in connection with *Monumenta Musicae Byzantinae*.' . . .

Success continued along these lines and it was increasingly evident to the Academy that the Pilgrim grants, small though they necessarily were upon an admittedly tentative basis, had revealed or emphasized a real and pressing need in the advancement of humanistic studies. Accordingly when, in March 1957, the Trust sent in the last of the three promised grants, the Academy took courage and decorum in both hands and coupled its acknowledgement with 'the hope that the Trustees may feel moved to reconsider the termination of this grant when they receive the report at the end of the triennium'.

This plea was more than an Oliver Twist. As the grants had proceeded in 1955–7, Kilmaine and I in conversation had formulated with increasing precision the notion that the whole thing should be regarded essentially as a pilot-scheme for future Government action. If we could present the Treasury with a clearly substantiated need, complete with successful experimental treatment, our case for a permanent humanistic research grant outside the immediate purview of the overburdened universities would have been removed from the realm of postulate to that of proof.

Accordingly, following its final report (1957) to the Trust, the Academy was able to record that in the three years effective grants had been made to forty-one scholars; many of them young post-graduate research workers, but others more mature scholars for whom appropriate funds were not otherwise available.

In all cases the possibility of alternative sources had been explored by the Academy, and it could be affirmed that the allocations had been made with a proper economy to fill gaps in the present provision for research of this kind.

The general inadequacy of the funds available in the United Kingdom for research in the humanities has become increasingly apparent within the last ten years. In the light of this trend the Council of the Academy has been urgently considering the preparation of a more adequate over-all scheme for the encouragement of humanistic scholarship. . . . Meanwhile, the new stimulus which has been given to scholars in general by the Pilgrim Trust's generous subvention . . . has demonstrated anew the genuine character of the need.

The Pilgrim Trustees were 'greatly satisfied' and 'impressed', and promptly renewed their grant of £2,000 p.a. for three years, from January 1958 to January 1960.

But this was not the whole of the matter. In the confidential thinking of the officers of the Academy, shared as always with the private minds of the Pilgrim Trust, was the approaching possibility of carrying into effect the preparation of the over-all scheme for humanistic research mentioned in the last paragraph. Towards the end of 1957, under the leadership of Sir George Clark

as President, this possibility became a certainty. In December of
that year the Rockefeller Foundation placed a sum of money at
the disposal of the Academy to finance an inquiry into the facts
of the present situation in respect of humanistic research in the
U.K. and into the needs and remedies suggested by that situation.
More will be said of this inquiry below. Meanwhile, in view of the
hoped-for impact of such inquiry upon the mind of Government
when in the fullness of time a suitably documented report should
be ready for presentation, it was more than ever important that
the Pilgrim pilot-scheme should be maintained at full pressure.

In 1960–1, when the extended Pilgrim grants came to an end,
the expected report, involving as it did much travelling and research on the part of busy scholars, was not yet ready for top-
level judgement. There was a moment, but only a moment, of
hesitation, and in 1961 King's College, Cambridge, gallantly
came to the rescue with a research-grant of £2,000. But the need
for the renewal of the now-familiar pilot became no less pressing,
and in retrospect the courage displayed by the Secretary of the
Trust combined with (let us say) the rashness of the Secretary of
the Academy in confidently anticipating ultimate success by a
renewal of the Pilgrim grant was to be happily justified by the
event. After much oral discussion it was agreed that for the
second time the grant should be renewed at £2,000 p.a., for
1962–4. On this occasion, however, a new factor was introduced.
In earlier years the Pilgrim–Academy allocations had consisted of
relatively small sums for a relatively large number of projects. In
discussion it was now suggested that this policy dealt only with a
part of the problem. What of larger projects, which might be of
higher long-term value and would certainly demand grants on an
enhanced scale?

Various alternative schemes were considered in this enlarged
context. In the upshot, and in renewed consultation with the
Pilgrim Trustees, two major projects were accepted by the Academy for 1963 and 1964:
  (i) Towards the cost of the publication of a new and complete
       edition of the Works and Correspondence of Jeremy Ben-
       tham, under the direction of University College, London.
       . . . £750.
  (ii) Towards the cost of sorting, mounting, and listing the
       manuscripts from the Geniza of the Synagogue in Old
       Cairo and now in the University Library of Cambridge,
       under the direction of Professor D. Winton Thomas. . . .
       £1,250.

In thus envisaging the desirability of including 'major' as well as 'minor' schemes in the subvention of research, the Academy, supported by the Trust with undeviating loyalty and understanding, was now able at last to round off a long period of experiment and to turn its experience with confidence into the relatively permanent channels of its Government budget. To this major event in the Academy's history, and to the Academy's report, published in 1961, upon which the new policy was based, a proper attention may now be turned.

VI

RESEARCH: (ii) THE ROCKEFELLER REPORT AND ITS SEQUEL

In his critical and crucial Presidential Address of 4 July 1956, Sir George Clark drew attention to the random nature of the provision for research in the humanities and social sciences, and described it as 'a structure which is truly Gothic in its wealth of irregular detail'. In contrast, the coverage and cohesion of the bodies dealing with the natural sciences—notably, the Department of Scientific and Industrial Research, the Medical Research Council, and the Agricultural Research Council—were comprehensive and efficient. Of this disparity there was a growing consciousness, not only in the professionally academic circles of the Academy but also, as has been shown above, in the wider and more generalized purview of observers such as the Pilgrim Trustees. And now, in February 1957, a new and constructive phase in the formulation and presentation of the research-problem in respect of humanism and the social sciences was opened by conversation between F. D'Arms, of the Rockefeller Foundation, and the Academy's President. Mr. D'Arms was already aware of the Pilgrim pilot-scheme, then in its second year, and was in a receptive mood.

A letter from Sir George Clark to Mr. D'Arms at the London address of the Rockefeller Foundation on 27 February 1957 summarized and amplified the initial interchange, and may usefully be quoted in full:

Perhaps the best way for me to begin writing about the subject of our conversation on 19 February will be to put down my recollection of what passed between us.

You asked me about the grant of £2,000 a year for three years which the Pilgrim Trust made to the British Academy in 1955 'to assist scholars in the fields of the humanities and the arts to prosecute their research'. I said that I would arrange for the reports on the administration of this grant to be sent to you. I said that, in view of the limited amount of the grant, we had never expected to be able to produce the best possible list of recipients, but that we had succeeded in our hope of producing a good list and we had reason to believe that, if more money had been available, the list could have been considerably extended. The

4. Sir George Clark (President 1954–1958).

release from normal duties. The committee would compare the arrangements at present existing in this country with those in foreign countries, but it would not produce anything like a quantitative estimate of present needs in any branch of research. It would be concerned with surveying the needs only in as far as is required in framing proposals for the organisation of research. Its essential business would be to recommend to the British Academy what functions the Academy itself should aim at discharging in relation to this and what its policy should be in advising on the functions of other official and unofficial agencies. It was thought that if such an enquiry were undertaken it should, if possible, be completed in about a year. It would be best if the results could be published in a report (as brief as the subject matter allows) at the same time as the Academy's own annual report in July 1958. It was thought that this could scarcely be achieved unless the committee were able to have the services of an energetic and well-qualified secretary (of something like professorial standing), who could collect the necessary information, interview people whose advice was needed and do the necessary drafting. Such a secretary might have to be set free from other duties. He would, in any case, require remuneration and would incur some personal expenses. Although in the conversation between you and me nothing was directly said about such a plan as this, I hope I am not misinterpreting your point of view if I say that I hope your Foundation may be able to consider whether it could give any financial support to a proposal of this kind. The Council authorised me to write in this sense.

There is one other point which perhaps I ought to mention now. If the Academy appoints a committee on the lines suggested above, it will probably be an advantage if the committee can consider both the social sciences and the humanities, since the two touch one another at so many points. If your Foundation were able to support the enquiry, I should be glad to know whether it would prefer to support an enquiry into the humanities or one affecting the social sciences as well. I hope I have made it clear that the aim would be to make the relevant investigation in as compact a way and with as little expenditure of time and effort as could be compatible with a satisfactory result.

The Council wishes me to express its thanks for the interest you have taken in this matter. I need not say that I personally am really grateful for the interest you have taken and that I will most gladly provide any further information that may be needed.

After this letter, active negotiation both verbally and by letter between the officers of the Academy and the Rockefeller Foundation quickly shaped the scheme into a viable form. The Rockefeller representative continued at first to be Mr. F. D'Arms, but, on his departure to the Ford Foundation in August 1957, his place was taken by Mr. John Marshall. Continuity, however, was

grants have ranged from about £50 to about £150. I sa
experience had proved that there was a real need for such
we thought we had learnt how to distribute them.

I mentioned an important recent development in the pr
research funds, at the first level after graduation, by the State.
the decision of the Ministry of Education to stop the supplem
of college and university research awards and to provide inste
studentships which were to be awarded on the advice of a con
appointed by the Ministry. This had drawn attention to the c
between research organisation for the humanities and the systen
vailing in the fields of pure and applied science, medicine and ag
ture. For the latter the appointment of State studentships is to be r.
by the three great research departments under the Lord President o
Council (the Department for Scientific and Industrial Research,
Agricultural Research Council and the Medical Research Counc.
but, since there is no such body for the humanities, the Ministry
Education, which had no previous experience in matters of this kin
has undertaken the distribution. You asked whether the Ministry'
committee for this purpose could become the nucleus of a national body
performing functions resembling those of national bodies for research in
the humanities in France and other countries, but I said that this did
not appear possible and that, if there were to be any such body, it would
probably have to be quite differently constituted. I referred to my
annual address in 1956 to the British Academy in which I had reviewed
the position as it was before the Ministry's decision in regard to research
awards. A copy of this is enclosed. I mentioned another development
subsequent to the delivery of that address, namely that the financial
difficulties of the National Institute of Economic and Social Research
and the Royal Institute of International Affairs had been met, at least
for the time being, by grants from the Ford Foundation.

On 20 February, at the meeting of the Council of the British Academy,
I reported on the conversation which I have summarized above, em-
phasising that, although the British Academy is concerned both with
the social sciences and with the humanities, my conversation with you
had been limited to the humanities. The Council was of opinion that it
would be advisable, in view of the present juncture, to form a policy in
regard to these matters. It took the view that as there had never been
any survey of the provision for research in the humanities comparable
to those made by the Government committees at the end of the recent
war, such as the Clapham Committee on the Social Services and the
Scarbrough Committees on Oriental and Slavonic Studies, it would be
wise to begin by some such survey of the field of the humanities. They
favoured the plan of appointing a small committee to enquire into the
present arrangements by which research at all stages is provided with
finance, for such purposes as publication and the maintenance and
expenses of scholars including the expenses of travel, equipment and

not interrupted, and in December of that year the Academy was able to present its definitive proposal to the Foundation. The main bulk of the proposal should be put on record, and was as follows:

The Council of the British Academy has given its approval to a proposal for the preparation, printing and publication of a report surveying the existing organisation in the United Kingdom of the studies represented by the British Academy, with special reference to the public and private bodies which provide financial support. During the last two years it has become generally recognised that many of the bodies concerned with such research will need to seek financial support from sources to which they have not previously applied; but, in giving advice and assistance in such matters, the Council has found that there is a need for fuller and clearer information about the resources and functions of the existing organisations. There is also a need for some clear statement and discussion of the principles which govern their purposes and mutual relations. Recent changes, for instance, in the system of state subvention to graduate students in the universities have drawn attention to the absence of any machinery for the arts and social sciences comparable to that of the Department of Scientific and Industrial Research and the other official research councils.

The proposed report would deal with the subjects represented by the British Academy, or in other words with the subjects of higher study and research other than the natural sciences, which are similarly represented by the Royal Society. It would cover both the humanities and the social sciences. Although it is recognised that the problems of these two fields are dissimilar, especially in the matter of government assistance, and although some important organisations are confined to one field or the other, it has been found necessary to propose a survey covering both fields. There are two reasons for this: (1) there are institutions, including the British Academy itself, which make and receive grants of money and exercise a measure of control in both fields, so that the provision from either cannot be adequately discussed in abstraction from the other; (2) one of the purposes of the enquiry would be to consider where the line of demarcation should be drawn, and how far each field requires its own distinctive arrangements for official and private support.

The report would review the constitution, finance and operation of the existing agencies, taking account of their own views on their effectiveness or deficiencies. The needs of the various branches of research would be considered. Here the purpose would be not to make research programmes but to estimate the nature and scale of the projects for which support will be needed, and especially to indicate what major developments (such as new issues of major works of reference, or editions of correspondence on a scale which is at present too great for the resources of the bodies concerned) are at present impracticable because of the lack of funds. Attention would also be paid to needs of the kind which have been met during the past three years by grants to individual research-workers from the experimental grant administered by the British Academy for the Pilgrim Trust. Research carried on in the universities would not be excluded from consideration. The part played by international organisations, and the need for funds to enable the British participation in their projects to be made more effective, and also the support given from overseas, especially by Foundations, would be described.

Recommendations would be made for any new arrangements that may appear desirable, and in arriving at such recommendations the Committee charged with the preparation of the report would consider such examples in foreign countries as may provide suitable guidance. The functions of the British Academy itself would be amongst the subjects considered, since it has the duty of examining and submitting to the Treasury certain classes of applications for Government subsidies to research-organisations. For this reason it is judged that the Committee should consist of Fellows of the Academy.

Proposed Organisation and Time-Table

It is proposed that the Academy should appoint six of its Fellows as a Committee, under the Chairmanship of its President or his delegate elected by its Council, with a well-qualified Secretary of good academic standing, not necessarily a Fellow of the Academy. The general working of this Committee would be similar to that of the Commission on Library Provision in Oxford which was financed by the Rockefeller Foundation in 1930, except for the position of the Secretary. The Secretary of the Oxford Commission was an officer of the University of Oxford released from his ordinary duties for this purpose, but the present staff of the British Academy does not include anyone who could be released for special duties and it will therefore be necessary to offer the Secretary not merely his actual expenses, but such a sum as would enable him to forgo his ordinary emoluments or compensate his employers for the loss of his services. This amount would, of course, depend on his circumstances and standing.

The work would be centred in London and the British Academy would provide the necessary accommodation. Clerical assistance would have to be specially engaged. It is proposed that the work should be carried out in four stages.

In the first stage the Committee would hold such meetings as were necessary for settling the programme. The Secretary, in consultation with the Chairman and with the participation of members of the Committee when advisable, would collect information in the United Kingdom, the chief sources of which would be first the available printed matter and secondly correspondence and interviews with the relevant bodies. The information so obtained would be digested and circulated to the Committee, which would continue to meet as required.

The second stage would be devoted to supplementing this information with the relevant foreign comparisons. It is not at present expected that any countries would have to be visited except the United States, Canada, France and possibly Holland and Western Germany. It is hoped that in all cases brief visits would suffice. The Committee would not be able to travel as a body, since it would be impossible for all the members to be away from their usual posts at the same times. The plan would therefore be for the Secretary to carry out the visits in the company of one or more members of the Committee, the members for the several visits being chosen with regard to their special qualifications and interests. Information acquired in the second stage would be dealt with as in the first.

The third stage would be that in which the Committee would consider its recommendations. The Secretary would provide the necessary drafts and other papers, and the Committee would meet as frequently as possible.

The fourth stage would be that of publication. It is understood that the Rockefeller Foundation would not contribute to the cost of printing or publication, for which the British Academy would be responsible.

Since the conditions of the problem are liable to unexpected changes, it is in the highest degree desirable that there should be no unavoidable delays; but it is impossible to fix definite dates for starting and finishing until the Committee is actually set up. It is, however, possible to form an idea of the duration of the work, and it seems reasonable to aim at sending a report to the printer some 16 or 17 months after starting.

Cost of the Survey

The amounts which would be needed for the various purposes are estimated to be as follows:

Expenses of Members of Committee attending 25 meetings in London	£1,000
Additional London Expenses of Chairman	200
Remuneration of Secretary (up to 200 days)	1,000
Expenses of Secretary	1,400
Expenses of Travel away from London	1,000
Clerical Assistance and Incidental Expenses	1,400
	£6,000

On 29 January 1958, the Secretary of the Rockefeller Foundation informed the Academy that the proposal had been accepted by the Foundation's Executive Committee, and that the sum of £6,000 would be at the disposal of the Academy during the period

ending 31 December 1959 (later extended to 31 December 1961), as a contribution towards the costs of a survey of research in the humanities and social sciences in Great Britain.

Of its own volition the Academy had been allowed little enough time in which to fulfil its considerable task, and action followed quickly. By March 1958 its 'Rockefeller Committee' had been constituted, consisting of Professor R. I. Aaron, Professor Bernard Ashmole, Professor E. R. Dodds, Professor (Sir) Goronwy Edwards, Professor A. Ewert, Sir Ivor Jennings, and Dr. Kathleen M. Kenyon, with the President as chairman. Professor Sir Isaiah Berlin was later co-opted to the Committee. Sir George Clark, who had borne the brunt of the initial negotiations, ended his appointed term as President of the Academy in July 1958, and, whilst remaining a member of the Committee, was succeeded in office by Sir Maurice Bowra who, after the first three meetings (on 25 April, 9 July, and 29 July), conducted the Committee's busy proceedings and actively directed the preparation of the Report. The Academy was meanwhile happy in discovering and appointing Mr. R. H. Hill as the investigation's full-time secretary. Until 1 July Mr. Hill had been Librarian and Secretary to the Trustees of the National Central Library, and brought both knowledge and experience to his new post.

The resulting report on *Research in the Humanities and the Social Sciences* (120 pp.) was approved by the Council of the Academy on 15 February 1961, and was published in September of that year for the Academy by the Oxford University Press. But before the sequel is recorded, it may be of interest to summarize the general course of the Rockefeller Committee's enquiry. (Its official title was 'Survey of Provision for Research in the Humanities and the Social Sciences, Rockefeller Grant'.) Eighteen meetings were held, the first on 25 April 1958, and the last on 9 February 1961.

1st meeting. The scope, organization, and time-table of the enquiry were discussed on the basis of a proposal already drafted [and later accepted in the amended form cited above]. The Chairman of the Committee and its Secretary were authorized to draft the necessary estimate and to forward it to the Rockefeller Foundation.

2nd meeting. Reported that the Foundation had approved an estimate of £1,500 for expenditure in the calendar year 1958. Further consideration was given to the field covered by the enquiry. It was agreed that the information sought should cover research at all levels from first degree onwards; and (*inter alia*) the existing financial and material provision and facilities, and the procedure and machinery through which grants were considered and made. Existing documentary material should be secured and copies circulated where desirable to the Committee.

A preliminary list of bodies to be approached was agreed. It ranged from H.M. Treasury to the Research Councils, principal libraries and museums, central university bodies, Public Records, etc., the Ministry of Education, the major foundations, the university presses and the Publishers Association.

3rd meeting. The division of interests as represented by the members of the Committee was considered. Visits abroad to supplement information from the U.K. were tentatively planned and allotted to members of the Committee. The list included the U.S.A. and Canada, France, Holland, and Western Germany and Switzerland, and other possible visits were mentioned, subject to enquiry. Drafts of a general letter to grant-giving bodies, and of a letter and questionnaire to small foundations, were amended and approved, and the general lines of letters to Vice-Chancellors, presses, and H.M. Treasury approved.

4th meeting. The arrangements for visits abroad were reviewed, and possible additions to the list considered.

Sir Maurice Bowra and Sir George Clark had visited H.M. Treasury to outline the nature and scope of the Academy's survey, and the proposal had been sympathetically received. Accordingly, the invitations to grant-giving bodies, etc., would be despatched forthwith and the press would be informed. Office accommodation had been secured at 3 Belgrave Square.

5th meeting. The field of enquiry was further considered, with special reference to the inclusion or exclusion of social studies from the Committee's purview. Further consideration would be given to this matter as the investigation proceeded. An encouraging memorandum had been received from Professor (Lord) Robbins. Further consideration was also given to the proposed visits to the U.S.A. and Canada, and Mr. John Marshall would be consulted. A rough outline of heads under which information might be sought abroad was discussed.

6th meeting. Sir Gilbert Flemming, Permanent Secretary of the Ministry of Education, and Dr. (Sir) Peter S. Noble, Chairman of the Committee on Grants for Research, had been interviewed, and reports were attached. Visits to the U.S.A. and Canada were finalized. Communications and questionnaires to the smaller foundations and other suitable bodies would now be dispatched.

Letters from the Pilgrim Trust and the Deputy Director-General of the British Council were laid before the Committee.

7th meeting. (Sir) Frank Francis of the British Museum gave an outspoken account of conditions in his Museum. Whilst in theory research was accepted as a normal and proper occupation of its academic staff, in practice opportunity was negligible.

Further details, prepared in part with the help of Mr. John Marshall, were given in regard to the forthcoming visits to the U.S.A. and Canada, and to Western Germany, Switzerland, Holland, Belgium, and France, but it was agreed that visits to Eire, Italy, the Scandinavian countries, and Spain would prove unnecessary, and that any useful evidence should be sought by correspondence.

8th meeting. Sir Keith Murray, Chairman, and Sir Cecil Syers, Secretary of the University Grants Committee, gave their views on a number of points. In particular, it was observed that 'Social Studies may well prove one of the most useful bridges between Science and the Humanities; but whereas the Department of Scientific and Industrial Research can allot funds for a special requirement (not necessarily in connection with a university) there is nothing to take its place in the Humanities. The U.G.C. feel strongly that there should be an impartial superior body to help over the latter. . . . The U.G.C. has no machinery for encouraging and making direct contributions to special projects.'

In regard to the proposed visits to the U.S.A. and Canada, the President of the American Council of Learned Societies had proved most willing to assist. The Secretary was asked to circulate to the Committee a memorandum received from Professor Aaron on provision for research in the humanities in Italy.

9th meeting. Representatives of the Association of University Teachers—Professors S. T. Bindoff, Professor A. Carey Taylor, and Mr. J. E. G. Utting—were interviewed. They emphasized the need for facilities for research and for publication, down to thesis level.

Final arrangements for the visits to the U.S.A. and Canada, Western Germany and Holland, and France were reported.

10th meeting. Mr. C. H. Roberts, Secretary to the Delegates of the University Press, Oxford, was interviewed. He dealt with the general scope of the Press as a self-financing non-profit-distributing body. It had no publicized policy with regard to subsidies, but it undertook important projects which ordinary firms do not. There were very few cases in which a suitable book would not be published irrespective of subsidy. The Press would hope to be able to finance learned publication with the profits of its other departments.

A verbal report was made by Professor Ewert on the visit carried out by himself, Professor Aaron, Dr. Kenyon, and the Committee's Secretary to the U.S.A. and Canada.

11th meeting. A memorandum was received from the British Records Association.

Reports on visits to Holland and West Germany were presented by Sir George Clark and Professor Dodds respectively.

The Committee considered future procedure on the basis of a memorandum from the Chairman entitled *Some Main Questions*; and the following members agreed to draft, for consideration at the next meeting, memoranda on certain paragraphs in the Chairman's memorandum:

Sir George Clark on 'A central body to assist research'.
Professor Aaron on 'Opportunities for research: study leave'.
Professor Dodds on 'Publication'.
Dr. Kenyon on 'Neglected subjects'.
The Chairman on 'Institutes for Higher Learning'.

12th meeting. Written reports on the visits (*a*) to the U.S.A. and Canada and (*b*) to France were given general discussion. It was agreed that fuller information should be sought as to the bearing of tax laws on the provision of funds for research.

Memorandum on points raised by the Chairman at the previous meeting had been circulated and was discussed.

13th meeting. Professor W. J. H. Sprott, Professor of Philosophy at Nottingham, was interviewed in regard to the needs of sociological research. He observed that, in addition to funds currently received from foundations and other sources, there was a need for a more academic body to advise Government and to co-ordinate work. There was certainly a need for closer liaison between universities and the Social Survey (department of the Central Office of Information). Professor Sprott subsequently submitted a summary survey of the current teaching of Sociology in British universities. A memorandum by Professor Dodds on 'Subsidies for Publication', and letters from the University Presses of Cambridge, Manchester, and Liverpool and from the Marc Fitch Fund were also discussed.

14th meeting. Evidence supplementing a circulated memorandum was given by Dr. J. N. L. Myres, President, and Professor W. F. Grimes, Past-President of the Council for British Archaeology. It was emphasized that, with sufficient further funds, the Council was in a special position to give discriminating support to archaeological publication, whether in periodical or in monograph form. Such support could be instrumental in improving standards. It was felt, too, that an over-all body such as the Council could usefully sponsor selective excavation outside the salvage-work directed through the Ministry of Works, and could supply qualified research assistants, and draughtsmen, comparable to the secretarial assistance given to an historian.

The Committee also considered the nature, length, and form of its report, on the basis of a scheme drawn up by the Chairman and circulated beforehand.

15th meeting. Sir Thomas Kendrick and Dr. D. B. Harden attended and discussed with the Committee the subject of Museums. It was affirmed that no specific instructions were laid down as to research by British Museum officials in Museum time, though research was encouraged if it was related to departmental work. With increasing exigence on the part of the general public, however, little office-time remained for serious research. In provincial museums the remuneration of keepers was usually insufficient to attract men of outstanding capacity for research. Moreover, the unsatisfactory conditions in smaller museums were worsened by small staffs, inadequate salaries, lack of expert knowledge on selection and other committees, and often lack of ready library facilities. In spite of these disabilities, keepers were expected to organize local archaeological projects which incidentally provided the main training-ground for young archaeologists. Where education committees and officers were in control, museums tended to become geared to the school-teaching standard rather than to be regarded as research institutions.

The Committee received first drafts of sections of the Report already allocated, and a time-table for future procedure was agreed.

16th meeting. The Editorial Sub-Committee had met at Wadham College, and available chapters and appendices of the report had been considered and amended. The Committee continued this process, and expressed the view that financial information, e.g. upon Government and university expenditure on research, should be included and would facilitate some comparison with the sums expended for science and technology by the D.S.I.R., etc. Otherwise the arrangement and contents of the report were now drafted.

17th meeting. The Chairman reported verbally on a further meeting of the Editorial Sub-Committee at Wadham College. It was agreed to ask the Academy for leave to print the report in proof form forthwith.

18th meeting. The draft report of the Committee, now in printed slip-proofs which had been circulated, was considered and amended. It was decided that a few suggestions made by members of the Academy's Council should be collated in consultation with the Chairman of the Committee, and that a paged proof should then be circulated to all members of the Committee. The first printing should be 2,000 copies, and the President and Secretary of the Academy would consider distribution. Publication would take place in September 1961.

Since the *Report on Research* is available, little need be said here about its recommendations. Very briefly they were as follows:

1. The position of research in the Humanities and the Social Sciences would be more satisfactory if there were some authority which could allot funds, as the Department of Scientific and Industrial Research does, for special requirements, not solely or necessarily in the universities.

2. The existing provision for study leave and travel grants for research workers is uneven and in many respects inadequate. Suggestions for improvement were offered.

3. Certain types of research work (examples given) cannot be published without subsidies, and subsidies are also needed for the publication of learned journals and for collective projects.

4. The learned societies, whose work is essential for the status of our national learning and culture, are finding it increasingly difficult to exercise their essential functions. In particular, they need assistance to maintain their central offices and their libraries, to provide staff for them, to maintain their journals, and to provide for visits by Commonwealth and foreign scholars.

5. In view of the many needs of libraries, some national agency is needed to finance a survey of existing library facilities in order to consider in what ways improvements in the provision of books, buildings, and staff could be made, to what extent overlapping

could be avoided, and how far the existing national system of library co-operation could be reinforced and expanded.

6. In museums, grants are needed for additional staff, for study leave, for travel, for excavation, for publication of catalogues, etc., and for photographing, microfilming, etc.

7. In two groups of subjects research is hampered by special difficulties. The first consists of subjects which, despite their intrinsic importance, for economic or other reasons do not at present attract more than a very few students. The group includes many modern and some ancient languages and literatures; it also includes the history and archaeology of such vast and increasingly important areas as India, Africa, and the Middle East. The second group consists of subjects which are still incompletely or insufficiently recognized in British universities, for example the History of Science, Musicology, Sociology, and General Linguistics. The remedy in respect of both groups is to build up a few strong centres for each subject with adequate research facilities and sufficient research studentships.

8. In respect of Archaeology, the chief needs are an increased number of university posts, especially junior posts, and a central fund from which grants can be made for excavation, publication, and other archaeological projects of a less expensive nature, capital expenditure by the British Schools, scientific reports, and expenses of part-time and free-lance archaeologists.

9. There is similar need for the training of social anthropologists and for financial support for research programmes in Social Anthropology.

10. To attract new entrants of high quality to the study of Sociology, more established posts are required, and finance is needed especially for teams engaged on field-work.

11. Specialized institutes can perform an important service in the creation and preservation of standards; but the degree of need for them varies. In subjects involving field-work, not easily combined with full-time teaching, and in those requiring extensive technical equipment and assistance, the case for them is very strong. In the older literary subjects the need is generally less urgent.

These are bare headings; the Report as a whole is both informative and cogent and its seventy-two pages (plus appendices) should be read as a whole.

And now for action. This was taken with all decorous promptitude by a delegation of the Academy consisting of Sir George Clark, Professor E. R. Dodds, and the Academy's Secretary, under the leadership of the President, Sir Maurice Bowra. Ricocheting off Norman Brook (head of the Civil Service), we found our destination in the room of Henry Brooke (now Lord Brooke), then Financial Secretary of the Treasury. The ensuing conversations were lively and informal. Our Report had been studied and its main contentions were accepted. When our primary recommendation came up for discussion—the need for some over-all authority for the distribution of funds—Mr. Brooke took the point with immediate understanding. It had been put by us with a proper impersonality and a desire to avoid any imputation that we were primarily concerned with our own interests. But Mr. Brooke at once made a pertinent and important suggestion: that there was in fact no need to create a new independent central body for this task, since the work could be done equally well by the British Academy itself with considerably less expense in overheads. One reservation only was made: that provision for the Social Sciences was already under consideration in another context, and that the Academy for purposes of grants should adhere solely to the pure 'Humanities'. We went away, however, with a clear impression that something would be done to implement the main body of our Report. No sum was mentioned, but that was a formality for negotiation at a lower level.

Some weeks went by and nothing happened. The time approached for Sir Maurice Bowra's last Presidential Address, due for 11 July 1962. At last I hastened down to the Treasury and put the matter with force and urgency. It was now or never. Without a specified grant in his pocket, our President, and indeed the Financial Secretary, would be restricted on this cardinal occasion to the indignity of mere air and bathos. The dramatic moment had arrived to pin immediate and proper substance to the Financial Secretary's expressed goodwill. . . . I left the Treasury with an initial grant of £25,000 a year and the avowed intention of a rise to £50,000 at an early date. Today (1969) it is £65,000, and Government grants to research in the Humanities are an established feature of the Academy's budgets. The work begun with the aid of so much foresight by the Pilgrim Trust, and developed in collaboration with the Rockefeller Foundation with so much acumen by Sir George Clark in his Presidency, had been brought to a triumphant conclusion almost on the last day of Sir Maurice

Bowra's vigorous tenure of that office. It had been a happy episode with a happy and fructuous ending.

A word may be appended as to the machinery adopted from
the outset by the Academy in distributing awards from its
Government Research Fund. Grants for research from non-
Government funds are allocated in parallel fashion, and there
is close cross-reference in the administration of the two sources.

The availability of the Government fund is made known
annually to all Fellows and to the universities and principal
museums. These channels are supplemented by limited public
advertisement.

As they reach the Academy, applications are liberally summarized for distribution in first instance to a representative
Research Fund Committee which, after rejecting manifestly
unsuitable applications, dispatches the remainder to appropriate
Sections or other committees for careful scrutiny and categoriza-
tion. The categories at present used (with sub-divisions) are A and
B, both indicating viable schemes though with differing priorities,
and C, indicating absolute rejection. Commentaries are added
where thought desirable.

The third stage is to refer back the Sectional and other reports
to the Research Fund Committee for semi-final selection, having
regard to the total sum available for distribution. In this selection,
priority is given to a limited number of 'major research projects',
designated as such by Council and generally administered
directly by the Academy. Finally, the Committee's selection is
carefully reviewed by Council and, with agreed amendments
(if any), duly promulgated. The final list may, on the average,
approach fifty per cent of the viable applications.

It may be added that, from the Research Fund distributed on
these lines, the sum of £4,000–£5,000 has been set aside for allocation to selected 'primary' or 'central' research-periodicals, in
the Nuffield tradition (above, pp. 24 ff.). This important allocation has been made by a committee comprising the Chairmen
of Sections and the President of the Academy.

VII

OTHER BENEFITS NOT FORGOT

Whilst the gates of the great Foundations, and at last the portals of the Treasury itself, were opening to us in the friendly fashions which have been recounted above, lesser but still valued benefactions were gradually increasing the Academy's utility and, incidentally, its prestige. In the present chapter are collected such gifts of this kind as have accrued to the Academy during the twenty years now under review.

(i) THE STEIN–ARNOLD EXPLORATION FUND

Within the small Christian cemetery in Kabul, capital of Afghanistan, lies the grave of Sir Aurel Stein, K.C.I.E., F.B.A., who, having at last achieved a long-frustrated ambition to reach Afghanistan, died shortly after his ultimate arrival there in 1943 in the garden of the American Legation and in his 81st year. He was a small man who had suffered physically in his incessant Asian travels, but he was a legend. I recall how, when he was momentarily in London during the 'thirties, I lured him into my classroom and he addressed my students. He deeply impressed them all, very much as in an earlier age Field-Marshal Lord Roberts used to impress those with whom he came into contact: as a man of infinite courtesy with the heart of a lion in disproportionately small compass. They were great *little* men, both of them.

Stein had long been anxious that after his death his exploratory work should be continued in central Asia, preferably with some special reference to Greek impacts. He also wished that his 'much beloved and valued friend', Sir Thomas Arnold, K.C.I.E., F.B.A., one-time Professor of Arabic in the University of London, should be associated with him in his bequest: hence its 'Stein–Arnold' title. The will became formally operative at the end of 1948, but did not reach the Council in final form until 1949 and falls therefore within the period of this record.

The principal conditions attached to the bequest were:

(*a*) that the capital should be retained by the British Academy and that its income should be applied for 'the encouragement of research on the antiquities or historical geography or early history or arts of those parts of Asia which come within the sphere of the ancient civilizations of India, China, and Iran, including Central Asia, . . . so that special consideration shall be paid, if possible, to research of this character bearing upon the territories comprised in the present Kingdom of Afghanistan including the region of ancient Bactria and in the north-western frontier region of India, towards which the Testator's scholarly interests were drawn all his life'.

(b) Sponsored research should be carried out (so far as possible by exploratory work) by British or Hungarian subjects, the latter term including all persons, native or naturalized, 'of the territories which belonged to the Crown of St. Stephen in or before 1917'.

(c) The purposes of the Fund should include the encouragement and assistance of capable students and scholars by means of scholarships, travelling fellowships, or otherwise in such manner as might be determined by the administering body: i.e. by a Stein–Arnold Committee appointed and controlled by the Council of the British Academy.

(d) Special care should be taken to secure the timely and complete publication of the results of investigations effected with the help of the Fund. The publication should always take place primarily in English.

(e) Within the limits prescribed by this Scheme, the Council of the Academy should have full power from time to time to make, alter, and rescind regulations for the management of the Charity.

It may be added that, at the time of writing, the income of the Fund is approximately £700 p.a.

In fact, the last major project undertaken by Stein was not in the regions named but in Iraq, where in 1938 and 1939, stimulated by the dramatic results of Père Poidebard's air-surveys of the Roman frontier-region in Syria, he had begun a similar enterprise with the help of the Royal Air Force and the Iraq Petroleum Company. Brief accounts which appeared promptly in the *Geographical Journal* and elsewhere showed something of the potentialities of the investigation; and in the disturbed years between 1939 and his death at Kabul, Stein prepared a fuller manuscript with a view to ultimate publication. Before leaving on his last journey he tried to extract a promise from his friend Lieut.-Col. Kenneth Mason, then Professor of Geography at Oxford, that he would undertake to arrange for the publication of this manuscript. 'My answer', writes Colonel Mason, 'was that he was a wicked old man to go rollicking off into the blue at the age of 80 and to leave a comparative ignoramus to "clear up the mess". But he had the knack of persuasiveness very highly developed!'

Subsequent examination of the manuscript and of such of its illustrations as had survived the war years showed that in fact they were not in a condition for publication, and both Colonel Mason and others of Stein's friends felt that, had the author lived, he would have been of the same mind. Further field-work and a more leisurely assessment were demanded by the range and importance of the subject and by changing perspectives. The Academy and its Stein–Arnold Committee were happy in persuading Mr. David Oates, then Fellow of Trinity College, Cambridge, and later Director of the British School of Archaeology in Iraq, to give a new substance to 'the lost traveller's dream'; and between 1954 and 1958 Oates made a fresh survey, fortified by excavation, of sites in northern Iraq, using the Stein–Arnold Fund for the purpose. The very considerable results of this project were published for the Academy as *Studies in the Ancient History of Northern Iraq*, 1968.

After provision for this work of piety, the Stein–Arnold income was used for a variety of relevant purposes. These included first a contribution of the available accumulated income of the Fund to the limited excavation of the immense metropolitan site of Pushkalavati, on the Peshawar plain of West Pakistan. The excavation was carried out in October–December 1958 by the Academy's Secretary in collaboration with the Pakistan Government, and was published for the Academy and that Government as Mortimer Wheeler, *Charsada: a Metropolis on the North-West Frontier*, 1962. Secondly, in 1961–3, maximum grants were made to the excavations then being carried out by Mr David Stronach for the new British Institute of Persian Studies on the site of the Achaemenid capital of Pasargadae. Thirdly, in 1964 grants were given to Dr. F. R. Allchin towards the cost of excavation on the site of the Indo-Greek and Kushan town of Shaikhan-Dheri, near Charsada, West Pakistan; and to the Oxford University Expedition to the lapis lazuli quarries of Badakhshan in north-eastern Afghanistan. Fourthly, in 1966, a contribution was given to Mr. David Oates towards the cost of further excavation at Tell al-Rimah in northern Iraq, and to the Cambridge University Expedition to Seistan in southern Afghanistan. In 1967, an additional grant was made to Mr. Oates for Tell al-Rimah;

and it was decided to advertise a Stein–Arnold Travelling Fellowship, tenable from 1 June 1968 to 31 May 1969. In 1968 this Fellowship (£700) was awarded to Dr. Clare Goff for her field-study of the prehistory of Luristan and the cultural background of the Luristan bronzes.

(ii) THE ALBERT RECKITT ARCHAEOLOGICAL FUND

In December 1949, some six months after his assumption of office, the new Secretary of the Academy received a warming communication from his old friend Professor S. R. K. Glanville, F.B.A., then Professor of Egyptology at King's College, Cambridge, but writing as a Trustee of an archaeological trust established under the will of the late A. L. Reckitt, a name familiar to the business world in contexts such as Reckitt's Blue and Colman's Mustard. Mr. Reckitt's interests, however, had not been confined to successful commercial operations. His more personal concerns ranged widely over natural science and archaeology, and in the 'thirties he had contributed to the setting up of the new Institute of Archaeology in the University of London. Ten years later, when he drafted his will, he made provision for a number of trusts, which included one for archaeology. This 'technical trust' was Glanville's special concern in the guise of trustee adviser.

The Reckitt Trustees on the 13 December 1949 decided (on Glanville's advice) to offer the Archaeological Trust to the British Academy, if that body was prepared to accept conditions agreeable to the Trustees. Inquiry showed that these conditions were of an entirely liberal and acceptable kind; indeed the Academy was to have 'the widest discretion in administering the fund', both as to capital and as to income, although it was understood that sympathetic attention would be paid to the known wishes or tastes of the Founder. The principal guide-lines were (in simplified form) as follows:

(a) The income of the Trust Fund should from time to time be applied for the promotion of learning and education in the field of archaeology, in such manner as the Academy should think fit.

(b) In particular, grants might be made from these moneys for the exploration of ancient sites in any part of the world with a view to increasing knowledge of early civilizations and the history of mankind, and for the preservation and exhibition of objects discovered by such exploration and the publication of the results thereof.

(c) Grants might also be made for the purpose of increasing or contributing towards the emoluments and awards of professors, teachers, and research-workers in archaeology at any university in the United Kingdom;

(d) Also as contributions and donations for the purpose of archaeology to the funds of any university or other recognized institute or body of persons in the United Kingdom conducting archaeology, or of British Schools established in other countries.

(e) Grants might also be made for acquiring sites for, and erecting, maintaining or endowing any building in the United Kingdom to be used or already used for the promotion of research, learning, and education in archaeology;

(f) And generally for doing all such things as the Academy in its uncontrolled discretion might regard as conducive to the above purpose or purposes.

(g) It was the Founder's desire that the Ordinary Stock of Reckitt & Sons Ltd. should not be sold unless serious damage to the Fund should be apprehended if such Stock were retained.

Formal and final agreement between the Albert Reckitt Archaeological Trustees and the British Academy was reached on the 17 April 1950. At the transfer of funds, the annual income of the Trust was approximately £800 (subsequently £3,000) p.a. and there were cash assets in the neighbourhood of £3,000. The mild restrictions governing this Fund have enabled it to be used profitably over a wide range of projects in which 'research' and 'discovery' are not too narrowly defined and discriminated.

The Albert Reckitt Archaeological Fund is administered by the Council of the Academy on the advice of Section X. Its main functions are twofold: to finance a periodical (now biennial) lecture, and to subsidize approved projects, commonly though not necessarily involving field-work. The first lecture was given in November 1952 by Professor Stuart Piggott on *William Camden and the 'Britannia'*.

(iii) THE KENYON MEDAL FOR CLASSICAL LITERATURE OR ARCHAEOLOGY

Sir Frederic Kenyon, one of the early Fellows of the British Academy (1903) and subsequently its President and its Secretary, died in his 90th year in 1952. In his will he bequeathed to the Academy £250 to be invested for the provision of a medal to be made of any kind of metal and to be given biennially (or at longer intervals if necessary) to the author of some work relating to classical literature or archaeology which the Council shall judge to be worthy of it. Whether an award of this nature is or is not entirely in consonance with modern usage, the bequest was accepted with a proper appreciation as a dignified memorial of a distinguished Academician of another age, and a Committee was formed to consider the design and production of the medal.

It was agreed to recommend that the obverse should carry a head of Sir Frederic, and the reverse a papyrus roll with a quotation round it from Bacchylides.[1] The recipient's name would be engraved on the rim. The Committee proceeded to confer with the Deputy Master of the Mint in regard to details of production, cost, etc. It also examined at the Mint ('without enthusiasm') specimens of current medals, and proceeded thereafter to consult the Principal of the Royal College of Art, Mr. (now Sir) Robin Darwin. The Principal was found to be much concerned about the present low artistic level of the production of coins and medals, and welcomed our intervention. It was agreed that this low level was largely due to the mechanical methods involved in the use of the reducing machine and that the first step towards improvement would be for the artist's design to be produced on the same scale as the finished product and for the dies to be engraved direct from it.

For work of this kind the Principal was generously prepared to share the costs with the Academy from College funds at his disposal, and his collaboration was throughout of the closest. In consultation with Professor Robert Goodden, of the Royal College, the designing of the medal was carried out by Mr. Christopher Ironside, also of the College. The task was no easy one. Neither Goodden nor Ironside had known Kenyon, and the best available profile photograph was a faded print. Nor is the bronze bust in

---

[1] ἀρετᾶς γε μὲν οὐ μινύθει βροτῶν ἅμα σώματι φέγγος. *The splendour of merit does not decrease with the mortal body.*

5. The Kenyon Medal 1957.

the British Museum a convincing likeness. But after trial, and patient correction the final result is an admirable likeness (pl. 5), and the papyrus scroll, which gave the designers almost as much trouble as the head, is satisfactory.

By April 1957 the medal was at last ready, modelled in wax and cast in bronze, and was greeted by the expert eye of E. S. G. Robinson as 'a notable achievement, worth waiting for'. Later that year it was given to its first recipient, Sir John Beazley, C.H., F.B.A., and was thus launched upon a career of notable distinction.

(iv) THE DAWES HICKS LECTURE IN PHILOSOPHY

In addition to the bequest which established the Kenyon Medal, the year 1953 saw the maturing of three other bequests which continue to enrich the proceedings of the British Academy. The first of these had been anticipated in the will drawn up in 1932 by George Dawes Hicks who had for many years professed Philosophy in the University of London. For that earnest and somewhat other-wordly philosopher the present writer, after the lapse of nearly sixty years, still retains a vivid admiration, as for one who, against considerable odds, instilled in a young classical student at University College an enduring appreciation of the robust materialism of the early Greek physicists and the more cultivated niceties of their great successors, Plato and Aristotle. When therefore, as Secretary of the Academy, he received in May 1953 the news that the last of a number of annuitants under the will had now died and that an allotted share of the residuary estate had fallen accordingly to the British Academy, the occasion was something more than a merely financial interlude. It was with an almost nostalgic personal respect that he was able to inform the Academy's Council at its May meeting that it was about to receive from the Dawes Hicks Trust the approximate sum of £1,500 to provide a periodical lecture on 'subjects relating to the History of Philosophy, either ancient or modern'.

The first Dawes Hicks Lecture was given in June 1955, by the Revd. Professor F. C. Copleston on *Bergson on Morality*. The lecturers under the bequest are appointed by the Council of the Academy upon the recommendation of Section VII (Philosophy).

(v) THE CHATTERTON LECTURE

On 12 January 1953, Dr. Lionel Butler, Fellow of All Souls College, wrote to the Secretary of the Academy as an executor and trustee of the late E. H. W. Meyerstein, of Gray's Inn. Meyerstein, let it be recalled, was a remarkable, unpredictable character: minor poet, novelist, biographer, translator, and much besides, including, as a not very charitable friend remarked, the distinction of being 'the most unlikely member ever elected to the Athenaeum'. German Jewry, Harrow, and Magdalen went to his making; and from this amalgam emerged 'a man of letters whose sincere devotion to his craft is as patent as are his idiosyncracies and perversities'.

And now the Meyerstein trustees were instructed by his will

to set aside such sum as they consider adequate to provide for a public lecture to be given once a year by a lecturer who shall be under the age of forty, such lecture to be on the life and works of a deceased English poet and to be known as 'The Chatterton Lecture', such lecture to be given under the auspices of the British Academy or the Royal Society of Literature. . . .

I am writing to you first, [added Dr. Butler] to express the keen hope of all of us that the British Academy will be able to undertake the sponsoring of the Chatterton Lectures. I am empowered to say that we the executors and trustees are prepared to set aside for this purpose a sum of money that would under present conditions produce an annual sum of £100 net. . . .

Subsequent interchanges defined the term 'deceased English poet' as 'a deceased poet writing in the English language', and generously raised the annual income of the benefaction to £160 to include expenses such as printing.

The search for the annual lecturer—in the circumstances not always an easy task—was assigned to Section VI (Literature and Philology: Medieval and Modern), and the first choice fell happily and perhaps inevitably upon Lionel Butler, whose subject in March 1955 was, equally naturally, Meyerstein himself. In the course of a brilliant assessment of Meyerstein's quaint curiosity and erratic achievement, Butler incidentally answered any question that there may have been as to the origin of the 'Chatterton Lectures'. His author's

feeling and imagination were never more elevated than when Thomas Chatterton was their subject. He published his *Life of Chatterton* in 1930. Marked by small attention to 'readability', and by no deftness in apportioning material between text and footnotes, it is nevertheless of a quality and an insight far beyond those of the average standard biography. A reader who had not met the author might rightly suppose this book to have come from a scholarly, clever, and tireless mind. Meyerstein's friends knew that it was also a work inspired by passion. For Meyerstein was absorbed, indeed obsessed by Chatterton. He described him in poetry as his guardian angel, and he saw him in dreams —if not, as did Francis Thompson, in a waking vision. . . . To the end of his life he pursued his studies of Chatterton, and his heavily annotated master-copy of the biography he wrote now awaits a reviser in the Bristol [Central Library].

These under-forty lectures continue to adorn and enliven the Academy's proceedings.

(vi) THE WILLIAM HEPBURN BUCKLER MEMORIAL FUND

Of a more traditional kind was the Trust Fund of £1,500 given to the Academy in April 1953 by Mrs. Georgina G. Buckler, widow of William Hepburn Buckler, F.B.A., as a memorial to her husband, who had died in the previous year. Mrs. Buckler herself died very shortly afterwards, but her two daughters in April 1956 generously increased the capital sum by a thousand dollars, bringing the Fund approximately to £1,850.

W. H. Buckler was the son of a Baltimore physician but was born in Paris in 1867, and twenty years later went to Trinity College, Cambridge, where he read History and Law, winning the Yorke Prize in 1893 with an essay on 'The origin and history of contract in Roman Law'. He moved on to his ancestral Baltimore and to a miscellaneous career of law and diplomacy; but at the age of 43 he turned to archaeology and joined the Princeton expedition to Sardis as 'an active field archaeologist' with a strong bias towards epigraphy. Shortly after the outbreak of the 1914 War he returned to diplomacy and to London. After the War he resumed his archaeological interests and, under the influence of Sir William Ramsay, their scope extended to the epigraphy of Asia Minor and, egged on by his wife, to the Byzantine art of Cyprus. He moved his home-base to Oxford, took an Oxford doctorate and, in spite of his alien nationality, was elected in 1937 to a Fellowship of the British Academy. He died in 1952.

In consonance with Buckler's main historical or archaeological interests, Mrs. Buckler proposed, and the Academy accepted, that the interest of the fund should be devoted to the following three objects:

(a) Generally to assist or make possible research into the History and Antiquities of Asia Minor and Cyprus in the Classical Greek, Roman, or Byzantine periods;

(b) In particular and in pursuance of the said general purpose to assist and make possible travel in Asia Minor and Cyprus by suitable persons; and

(c) In pursuance of the said purposes to assist and make possible the preservation and publication of records of discoveries made and knowledge acquired.

Grants from this source are made by the Council on the recommendation of Section X (Archaeology). Sadly it is not always easy to discover an applicant who conforms with the exclusive chronological and geographical conditions of the Trust.

(vii) THE MACCABAEAN LECTURE IN JURISPRUDENCE

Amongst the Academy's endowed lectures there was none, prior to 1956, within the particular scope and responsibility of its Section of Jurisprudence. Accordingly, when in February of that year The Maccabaeans—a society mostly of Jewish professional men seemingly with a legal bias—informed the Academy that they were minded to mark the Tercentenary Year of Jewish re-settlement in this country by financing a periodical award or lectureship in the Society's name, the thought occurred that the opportunity might be taken to redress some part of this imbalance.

The Maccabaeans took the suggestion well, and on the strength of it dined the President (Sir George Clark) and the Secretary at the Trocadero. The capital sum available would finance a triennial lecture at current rates, and the subject would fall within the somewhat imprecise term, jurisprudence. In order that the Maccabaean Lectures might begin immediately, without waiting for accrued income, the cost of the first occasion would be a cash addition to the endowment. The Academy's Secretary approached Lord Evershed, Master of the Rolls, and the first Maccabaean Lecture was given by him on the subject of 'The Impact of Statute on the Laws of England', on 7 November 1956. It was a great success, and has been followed by others of no less distinction. Section VIII (Jurisprudence) was emerging from its chrysalis.

(viii) THE SARAH TRYPHENA PHILLIPS LECTURE ON AMERICAN LITERATURE AND HISTORY

In 1958–9 Dr. Carl Bode was the Cultural Attaché at the American Embassy in London, and found time to attend a number of lectures at the British Academy. Amongst them he missed any adequate attention to the American achievement, and we had conversations about this deficiency on a number of pleasant occasions. But Dr. Bode is a man of action, no less than of ideas, and in May 1958 he wrote briefly to me recalling these conversations and adding a positive and concise proposal:

... I wonder if you would ask the Officers and Council of the British Academy whether they would approve of a lecture every two years on American literature? I believe that you consider that an endowment of 5000 [later 4000] dollars would earn a suitable fee to the lecturer and the cost of publishing the lecture itself. If the Academy feels that this is a good idea, I should be glad to make an effort to find a patron for this scheme. ...

To this the Secretary of the Academy replied by return: '. . . I have already consulted my colleagues about the desirability of a Biennial Lecture on "American Literature and History", and the idea has been received with acclamation. The word "History" is inserted as a secondary title in case it should be found desirable to broaden the Lectureship in some particular context. But Literature would be the first priority . . . I feel that if the Lectureship is established it should be known as the "Bode Lectureship"!'

Bode rejoiced to hear the Academy's reaction, and added: I shall now knock on a good many doors. . . . But I do not believe that we should have a Bode Lecture; let it be named after any person or corporation so public-spirited and culturally-minded as to provide the needed money!'

Bode did not knock in vain. On his return to America he wrote (20 June 1960):

I am happy to report that the Ellis L. Phillips Foundation is interested in endowing the annual [biennial] lecture on American Literature and History. The chairman of the Foundation board . . . has asked me to write to you about the actual arrangements for the transfer of the 4,000 dollars. . . . He has suggested that the lectures be called the Sarah Tryphena Phillips lectures in memory of a great-aunt who was a teacher and writer of some renown during the late 19th and early 20th century. I feel, as I hope you do, that the idea is a good one. . . .

It was natural and proper to invite Professor Bode himself to give the first lecture of the series. He accepted, and on the 5 April 1961, addressed the Academy on 'The Sound of American Literature a Century Ago'. The lectures are a continuing success.

(ix) THE 'THANK-OFFERING TO BRITAIN' FUND

On 8 November 1965 an unusual ceremony took place at the Saddlers Hall in the City of London. A large party listened attentively to three speeches which can have left few of those present unmoved. In the Chair was Mr. Werner Behr, on his left sat Sir Hans Krebs, F.R.S. (winner of the Nobel Prize in Medicine and Physiology, 1956), and on his right Lord Robbins, President of the British Academy. Mr. Behr opened the proceedings with the words:

On behalf of the Committee of the 'Thank-you Britain' Appeal I welcome all of you. . . . With your permission I should like to tell you how the idea for this appeal originated. Some time ago the late Chairman of the Association of Jewish Refugees, Dr. Hans Reichmann, suggested that the former refugees should find an appropriate way to show their appreciation for the help accorded to them by this country at a moment of extreme anxiety and need. The idea was simply to say thankyou, without strings attached. Mr. Victor Ross, my co-Chairman, quite independently sent a letter to a leading newspaper, calling on his fellow refugees to remember what they had been through and how they found a haven. He received an enthusiastic response. . . . In our appeal letter we set a target of £40,000 to £60,000. I am sure you will be pleased to learn that we have been able to collect over £90,000. . . .

Handing a cheque to the President of the Academy, Sir Hans Krebs said:

This cheque and the efforts leading up to it are no more than a token, a small token, of the deep sense of indebtedness harboured by all of us who came to this country as refugees and were given here a new home —not merely a shelter but a true home. . . . No sum of money can adequately and appropriately express our gratefulness to the British people. . . . If it was force of circumstances and not our own choice which drove us out of the country of our birth, it was in many cases our free choice to take refuge and to settle in this country rather than in other parts of the globe. . . . What this country of our adoption gave us was not just a new home and livelihood. What we also found was a new and better way of life, a society whose attitudes to life were in many ways very different from what we had been accustomed to, and, I dare say, accustomed to not only under the Nazi rule. Coming from an atmosphere of political oppression and persecution, of hate and violence, of lawlessness, blackmail and intrigue, we found here a spirit of friendliness, humanity, tolerance and fairness. . . . We saw what Robert Browning said of his dog, 'strength without violence, courage without ferocity'. These are some of the characteristics of the soul of this country. It is this way of life with which some of us, I for one, fell in love. . . . It is a very small token of our gratitude which I now ask you, Lord Robbins, to accept in your capacity as President of the British Academy.

In his reply, Lord Robbins said:

The arrival here in the inter-war period of those who came from Nazi persecution was a painful symptom of what was going on in Central Europe—episode after episode culminating in outrages more frightful than have ever before occurred in civilized history. But it was a circumstance which brought great benefit in the world of scientific and humane learning, great benefit in music and the arts, and in technical and economic affairs, and not only here indeed but also throughout the remaining free world. A great book has yet to be written on the benefits of this exodus on the culture and civilization of the West. . . . Therefore it is for me a most deeply moving circumstance that, in addition to bringing these benefits, you should be making this thank-offering, and I am sure that my feelings will be universally shared when the news becomes widely known. It is we who should be expressing gratitude, not you. You have given twice. . . .

This interchange had been preceded by some months of discussion mostly between Mr. Victor Ross, Mr. Werner Behr, and Dr. Werner Rosenstock, representing the prospective donors, and the President and Secretary of the Academy. Gradually an acceptable scheme had taken shape, and was in the minds of all of us at the culminating ceremony recalled above. It was this: that the Fund should be used for two main purposes, (i) the establishment of an annual 'Thank-offering to Britain' Lecture, to be given by a lecturer of distinction (chosen by the Council of the Academy) upon some subject relating to 'Human Studies' widely interpreted in their bearing upon the well-being of the inhabitants of the United Kingdom; and (ii) a Research Fellowship similarly oriented, with alternative illustration in subjects such as sociology, economics, geography, history with a contemporary bearing, and international relations. The first lecture was given on the 6 July 1966 by Lord Robbins on the subject *Of Academic Freedom* and is published both separately and in the Academy's *Proceedings* for that year. The first Fellowship was awarded in October 1967 to Mr. John Allan Patmore, Lecturer in Geography at the University of Liverpool, for a scheme of research relating to leisure and the recreational use of public land. Mr. Patmore began by reviewing existing work in the field and by discussing the subject with relevant authorities. This led to the compilation of a book on land-use and leisure in England and Wales, which seeks to draw together many existing threads of research, supplemented by direct inquiry where the necessary material is not already available in appropriate form.

In due course Mr. Patmore turned from this to a more local and detailed aspect of his study, relating to the problem of the seasonal use of land for informal outdoor recreation in the Merseyside area. The result of this research should be highly relevant in planning the future provision for recreation and in considering the effective return of investment in different types of recreational facilities. Mr. Patmore's Fellowship was renewed for a second year to enable him to visit the United States and to carry his results to a stage suitable for publication, with relevant maps. In the U.S.A. he made a detailed study of the parks of the State of Ohio, and of the Huron–Clinton Metropolitan Authority. Shorter visits were made to Cincinnati, around the 'finger' lakes of northern New York, in southern Illinois, in the Cascades, on the Columbia plateau, and in the Howe Sound area of British Columbia. He took the opportunity of holding discussions with recreational geographers and conservationists at the four universities where he was invited to lecture. Work has also begun, in conjunction with a research-student who was awarded a Social Science Research Council studentship to study under Mr. Patmore's direction the Yorkshire Dales National Park, which should provide material for comparison.

(x) THE CATON-THOMPSON FUND FOR ARCHAEOLOGICAL RESEARCH

The Academy is happy to include in its Fellowship a lady who may be acclaimed as one of the first women to assume a leading and independent position in modern field-archaeology. Today (1969) the picture of feminine directors of remote archaeological expeditions or even schools of archaeology (Dr. Kathleen Kenyon at Jerusalem, Mrs. Diana Helbaek at Baghdad) is almost a commonplace. In 1929, when Dr. Gertrude Caton-Thompson excavated at Zimbabwe, in what was then Southern Rhodesia, it was a matter worthy of note, almost of awe. True, the tradition of redoubtable Englishwomen *in partibus* was itself no new one; after all, Lady Hester Stanhope is unique only in her own personality and that of the era in which she lived and domineered. But Dr. Caton-Thompson was no mere adventurer; she was a sober scientist who found her chosen and considerable problem in the African outlands and quietly got to work upon it, just as later she turned to another project of her careful choosing in a great desert valley of southern Arabia.

And now, years later, she has helped to ensure that other archaeologists, whether men or women, may find it a little easier to follow in her path or to strike out afresh. In 1968 Sir Kenneth Wheare, in his first Presidential Address, was able to

make special mention of a most generous gift which we have received from one of our own Fellows, Dr. Gertrude Caton-Thompson, who has presented the sum of £21,000 to the Academy for investment to provide grants for archaeological research. The purpose of awards from the Gertrude Caton-Thompson Fund is the furtherance of archaeological research whether in the field or in publication by scholars selected preferably, but not necessarily, from the Fellowship of the British Academy. This is a munificent addition to our resources and I know I speak for you all when I express to Dr. Caton-Thompson our warmest gratitude. It is also most encouraging to receive this expression of confidence in the work which the Academy is doing from one of our most distinguished and discriminating senior Fellows.

It is pleasant to add that the income of this welcome Fund is being devoted, with the ready approval of its donor, to the task of setting the Academy's new Society for Libyan Studies upon its feet: a project which was assured at the outset of the co-operation of the Libyan Government and should have a useful future in front of it when things settle down.

So, during twenty years, ten benefactions for specific but widely ranging purposes have come from non-Government sources to the hands of the Academy in its initiation or patronage of research. Combined with others already available, they constitute an encouraging basis for an expanding and varied programme of work. It is to be hoped that during the next twenty years the impetus may be sustained.

As an addendum to this chapter, reference may be made to the Annual Dinner at which, since 1956, the Academy has entertained itself and its friends. In 1952 it had celebrated the jubilee of its Royal Charter by dining at the Goldsmiths Hall in the City; and the subsequent generosity of its Fellow, Dr. A. L. Goodhart, encouraged the revival and continuation of this agreeable and useful *conventus*. For the purpose the Academy has been variously lodged by friendly hosts: in the hall of Gray's Inn, in the Grocers Hall, in the Banqueting House of Whitehall, and for many years in the Senate House of the University of London. Recently (1970) it has been happy to seek again the gilded shelter of the Goldsmiths.

VIII

EX AFRICA ALIQUID NOVI

THE writer of this record recalls how, many years ago, he and
his widely ranging friend O. G. S. Crawford, F.B.A., talked into
the night about the cultural shortcomings of our colonial regions
in Africa, particularly on the eastern side of that continent.
Neither of us had any immediate contact with those parts, but
both of us were aware how little that was new, in historical and
archaeological matters, ever emerged from them. If and when
links between France and Egypt, Persia, Afghanistan, Tunisia,
Algeria should cease there would in all those regions survive
some element of Western thought and collaboration in French
guise which might be expected to inform and stimulate the
consciousness of successor-nationalities. But what should we,
the British, have to show for ourselves amongst the upsurgent
peoples, for example, of the amalgam which we, most of us,
regarded vaguely as British East Africa? Precious little. Personal
exhaustion (for the moment) and absence of opportunity (for
several years) confined our problem to the pending-tray.

But only for a time. Chance ruled that one of us was to lie for
two years upon the sands of Africa; true, Africa of the Mediterranean rather than that of the tropics, but even the Western
Desert has about it something of the essential aroma of Africa.
And when after a few days in the Barbary town of Tripoli there
emerged upon the horizon a motley, friendly crowd of adven-
turers, ranging from shining purple negroes to leathery French-
men under the redoubtable Leclerc, a sudden sense of inner
Africa, of remote and fishful Chad, of which we knew pitifully
little, recurred to the mind of at least one observer.

Again there was a gap, but by the early 'fifties the Secretary of
the British Academy was again reviewing the cultural world
from his modest academic eminence. Again the lack of serious
or sustained cultural enterprise on the part of our colonial ad-
ministrators was patently manifest. And the time-limit was no
less patently shortening at a rapid pace.

By now the Secretary was by no means alone in this appreciation of the position. Opportunely at that moment, in July 1953,
an International Conference on African History was held at the

London School of Oriental and African Studies. Speaker after speaker (including the Academy's Secretary) urged action in the matter of the preservation and exploration of ancient sites and the salving of administrative and other records, which were fast vanishing or deteriorating. Relevant minutes of protest were steered, not without a certain helmsmanship, in the direction of the British Academy. They included the following:

1. The Conference was impressed by evidence that the outlines of African history, which was of such importance for African education, could be reconstructed by the co-operation of historians and archaeologists.

2. This would imply the adequate preservation of ancient and historical sites, monuments and documents, and the development of museums and public record offices.

3. Meanwhile the rate of destruction in all fields seemed to be steadily increasing. The revision of existing ordinances for the preservation of sites and other monuments, and for the control of excavation and the export of antiquities, should be accompanied by the formation of adequately staffed departments of antiquities.

4. Equivalent provision in respect of provincial and district records was equally urgent.

5. As an immediate step, it was desirable to establish an Institute of History and Archaeology in East Africa as a field training-school for students, somewhat on the lines of existing British Schools in Rome, Athens, Ankara, and elsewhere.

When these resolutions reached the Council of the British Academy at its meeting on the 11 November 1953, its ears were already attuned to receive them. A small sensible Committee on African Studies was promptly appointed 'to consider the matter and to take such preliminary action as it might think fit'. Encouraging contact was established with the Colonial Office, culminating in a visit by the President (Charles Webster) and the Secretary of the Academy to the Secretary of State for the Colonies, Oliver Lyttelton (now Lord Chandos).

At that meeting the general position was frankly and sympathetically discussed, with some special reference to East Africa but with cognizance also of wider issues, such as those presented by Aden and its Protectorate. The upshot was that the Colonial Secretary invited his visitors to set up a Committee, on which the Colonial Office would be officially represented, to advise him in matters relating to the history and archives of territories administered by his Office as such matters arose or could be foreseen. The invitation was welcomed by the Academy's Council on the 19 May 1954, and the following were nominated to constitute what was eventually called the 'Archaeological and Historical Advisory Committee for Overseas Co-operation': The President of the Academy, Sir Maurice Bowra, B. Cheeseman (the Colonial Office Librarian), Sir Gerard Clauson, Adrian Digby, D. L. Evans, Professor (Sir) H. A. R. Gibb, Dr. Kathleen Kenyon, L. P. Kirwan, the Revd. Gervase Mathew, Professor C. H. Philips, Sir Ralph Turner, and the Secretary of the Academy. This widely representative Committee replaced the more domestic African Studies Committee already set up by the Academy.

Almost simultaneously, Mr. Alan Lennox-Boyd (later Lord Boyd) succeeded Oliver Lyttelton as Secretary of State, and Sir George Clark followed Sir Charles Webster as President of the Academy. But there was no break on either side in this new phase of co-operation, and the Advisory Committee continued actively, both officially and less officially, to pursue its mission. In particular it occupied itself with the proposal voiced by the 1953 Conference referred to above, to establish a research school or institute for the promotion of historical and archaeological studies in East Africa; comprising Kenya, Uganda, Tanganyika, Zanzibar, and British Somaliland (this last subsequently dropped from the list).

Progress at first was inevitably slow. A great deal of unploughed soil had to be tilled before a revolutionary idea of this sort, unparalleled in the British colonial system, could be induced to take root. It may perhaps be claimed that a tiny beginning was made in August 1954, when the Academy's Secretary took the opportunity provided by his presidency of Section H of the British Association at Oxford to advertise both the need and its urgency as the theme of his presidential address. More important, in November of that year a preliminary statement of the East African situation, amplifying the resolutions of the 1953 Conference, was prepared by the new Advisory Committee and forwarded by the President of the Academy to the Colonial Secretary. But it is, I think, fair to say that the first practical move towards the fulfilment of the two primary requisites—provision for conservation and for research—was undertaken seriously in August 1955. And the real hero of the occasion came from outside the academic wall. He was the well-to-do leader of the East African sisal industry, Sir Eldred Hitchcock, with whom I came into contact in some forgotten fashion about this time and found instant friendship.

Hitchcock was a remarkable man. He began as Warden of Toynbee Hall, but during the First World War became associated with the wool-industry and in the Second World War he turned to East African sisal and became the sisal king, much to the benefit of the war effort. Latterly he turned also to tea-planting in East Africa and incidentally became a member of the Tanganyika Legislative Council. He was a man of many interests. He was for example an ardent collector of Persian pottery; two of his dishes are on my sideboard as I write, one of them—a classic piece—given to me when I opened an exhibition of his collection in Mayfair. He was above all concerned for the future of the past in Tanganyika, where he lived, and we often talked somewhat earnestly about the official and academic neglect of the history and monuments of the region. He became very interested in the scheme for an East African Research Institute, and promised appreciable financial help. His premature death in 1959, on the eve of the materialization of our Institute, forstalled this, but he had already given appreciable moral support to the project in the pre-natal stages of its growth.

Above all, in 1955 as a founder of the Tanganyika Archaeological Society he invited myself, together with my Oxfordian friend Gervase Mathew whose brother David had been the Roman Catholic Archbishop of East Africa, to visit the four territories, and particularly Tanganyika, as the new Society's guests. Throughout that August, with the ultimate backing of Lennox-Boyd at the Colonial Office and in conformity with an elaborate time-table, we sped from Entebbe to Nairobi, from Dar es Salaam to Zanzibar, from Government House to Government House, interrupted by a week or more in grass-huts on the famous Tanganyikan island of Kilwa Kisiwani where was carried out a small sample-excavation on the approved principles. At last we were getting down to earth. For the Kilwa interlude we were joined by Greville Freeman-Grenville—knowledgeable in East African history and numismatics—on delegation from his Government post. Our unremitting function was to interest the East African governments in our proposals and to prepare a programme of future operation. Everywhere we met everyone, and rapidly our plans took shape. One night we might, at Tanga in the semi-darkness of the Commissioner's open-air sundowner, harangue a miscellaneous and mildly amused crowd upon the virtues of East Africa's past, of which we were gradually if somewhat tumultuously becoming aware at first hand. On another night at Dar es Salaam the colourful Sir Edward Twining might throw a vast party in our honour and personally conduct an awestruck African police band in the illuminated seaward grounds of his Government House. (I have a particularly joyous memory-picture of the respectful efforts of the trombone-player to continue the manipulation of his massive machine whilst standing to attention and saluting H.E. as he quietly took over the baton.) And after the party we would sit with the Governor far into the night, as the empty glasses piled around us. For that is the way in which good work is done; not by loads of memoranda but by talk and talk and a little listening, savoured with a sufficiency of laughter and of the *soma* of the tropics.

From one of these sessions there issued a concrete proposal which was in fact not finally adopted but nevertheless constituted a useful stepping-stone in the long and unequal progress of negotiation. Twining readily grasped and indeed assumed our general plan for an East African Institute, and his urgent mind gave it an immediate and definitive shape which would, incidentally, ensure the location of the Institute's headquarters in his own treasured territory. On the coast forty miles north of Dar is Bagamoyo, once in the German period (before the First World War) the intended capital of Tanganyika at the coastal end of a main route into the interior and, as such, the point incidentally where Dr. Livingstone's body had left Africa. Some of the spacious buildings erected by the Germans were still standing in a semi-derelict state which would not prevent their adaptation to the purposes of an institute. The fact that, as we shortly discovered, twenty miles of the 'road' connecting Bagamoyo with Dar were almost impassable in all but the driest weather was no obstacle to our host: 'We'll put that right for you' was the immediate answer. For a time our unborn Institute became known as the 'Bagamoyo Project'.

It was interesting to observe how, after a variable start, the project became a sort of cultural prize for which the three main territories—Tanganyika, Uganda, and Kenya—began tentatively to advance competitive claims. In our own minds, the competition took a different form. Both historically and archaeologically East Africa might in the broadest sense be classified into two diverse and confronting regions: the coastal tracts and the deep interior. The former were rich in historical overseas contacts; with the Mediterranean, Persia, India, China. The latter, the interior, had little or no historical background prior to the nineteenth century save hypothetically for the rare penetration of trade-goods from the coast. Ideally, our new Institute should have two headquarters, one on the coast and another in the hinterland. For a time we did eventually have in fact a main headquarters at Dar and another at Kampala, capital of Uganda.

But that is to anticipate. In August 1955 our project, whether at Bagamoyo or anywhere else, was still basically a dream. We were beginning to sell the idea with some success in East Africa. When we got home, the whole scheme for a School or Institute of History and Archaeology in East Africa was carefully reviewed (November 1955) by the Academy's Advisory Committee in the light of our visit to East Africa and Sir Edward Twining's provisional offer. A detailed memorandum was approved and in the same month was accepted in principle by the Council for forwarding to the Colonial Secretary. By him it was circulated to the East African Governors with the observation that 'the case presented by the British Academy is rational and well-argued'. The replies of the Governors were reported by Mr. Lennox-Boyd in March 1956 to be 'of varying enthusiasm but they tend to the conclusion that Bagamoyo is the best site, even though a school there would have little support from the Government of Kenya and, in the financial field at least, probably only token support from the Government of Uganda . . .'. It may be noted that in principle the proposed Institute was now accepted both in Africa and in the Colonial Office, S.W. 1.

We were still, however, some distance from final ratification. There remained the ultimate assault on H.M. Treasury. On the strength of progress so far, a concise memorandum with a detailed estimate was submitted by the President of the Academy in June 1956 to Their Lordships for their vital verdict:

There is reason to expect that the Territories concerned will make some annual contribution; but for the remainder of the expenditure involved, the British Academy, in accordance with established policy in these matters, now ventures to approach Their Lordships for an annual grant-in-aid of £6,000. In doing so, I am able to say that it has the full support of the Colonial Office; and I may add that the Secretary of State for the Colonies has provisionally invited Sir Mortimer Wheeler to serve as the first Director of the new School.

There followed a protracted period of negotiation: constant notes and visits to the Treasury, sometimes with success a little nearer, sometimes further off than ever. The whole outcome of this very considerable project (in academic terms) was in the balance. On the Treasury side, Sir Alexander Johnston and C. G. Thorley were genuinely doing their best for us. But their Masters were against them. After all, this was that fatal phenomenon, a New Project, and the times were very bad.

On the other side, our prospective private donors in East Africa were dying or moving away or just losing heart. Months went by. Hitchcock himself was a sick man. On 13 January 1959 I wrote to him at Tanga:

I realise that these infernal delays in Whitehall have made things difficult, but having gone so far I personally am determined not to go back.

If necessary, I will fly out to Dar es-Salaam as soon as my Indian and Mediterranean expeditions release me, i.e. after April. It seems to me that active work on the spot, at Government House and elsewhere, will become essential. Meanwhile, no announcements should be made [of the likelihood of a forthcoming grant]—we don't want silly questions in the House before the Budget is passed. Indeed, it would be improper on all grounds to anticipate that event.

I know that you will be with me in my determination to go ahead, and if I do not see you here in April I should at least fall out of an aeroplane at Tanga on my way by a little later.

Looking back across the years I detect impersonally in that letter a hint of the obstinacy, which, I suppose, had helped to carry us through. There had indeed been discouragement enough. Alexander Johnston had been sorry to tell me that his Ministers were unable to supply an East African subsidy for 1957–8. Equally barren was 1958–9. But all this time we were still hammering away at the Treasury, and now and then the Colonial Office weighed in with a timely plea. Indeed my Treasury colleagues had, I think, begun themselves to take a truly personal interest in the affair. And at last on the 13 February 1959 a kindly whisper came through Lennox-Boyd that the Treasury had agreed to back our Institute in the forthcoming budget. For the financial year beginning in April 1959 the Academy received a grant of £6,500 for the East African project, and at the same time we were informed by the Tanganyikan Ministry of Finance and Economics that they had provided £2,000 in their 1959–60 estimates towards our new Institute's current expenses; Uganda followed suit with a grant of £1,000 and gallant little Zanzibar contributed £200. The ship was launched.

On 7 April 1959 Sir Eldred Hitchcock died at Tanga. How much of this news of fulfilment had reached him I was never able to ascertain.

The ship was launched but it remained to find both a crew and more ample rigging. As to the latter, the new President of the Academy, Sir Maurice Bowra, and the Secretary got to work at once. On our petition, the United Africa Company contributed £1,000 towards the cost of initial equipment, and the Nuffield Foundation generously financed research student-ships to the tune of £5,500. All this was a partial and welcome substitute for the more local benefactions which, some years earlier and under different economic conditions, had been fore-seen by Hitchcock. Meanwhile, a Governing Council, at first under the chairmanship of Maurice Bowra but subsequently under that of Mr. L. P. Kirwan (to whom the Institute has owed many years of wise direction), was set up and a policy-statement issued. The purposes of the Institute were defined as:

(1) To encourage and undertake research relating to the history and archaeology of East Africa, primarily but not exclusively in respect of the territories of Kenya, Tanganyika, Uganda, and Zanzibar.

(2) To award scholarships to British Commonwealth students and to provide other facilities for the studies indicated in (1) above.

(3) To publish from time to time a journal and monographs for the presentation of these studies.

(4) To co-operate freely with other research institutions in the territories named.

(5) To do all such other things (being in law charitable) as are incidental or conducive to the attainment of the foregoing purposes.

The search for a suitable Director pointed to Mr. Neville Chittick, who was, however, busily employed for the moment in the new post of Conservator of Antiquities in Tanganyika and would not be available for a year or so. To fill the gap, the Secretary's friend Richard Goodchild secured leave from his post as the Libyan Government's Controller of Antiquities in Cyrenaica and assumed the Directorship at Dar es Salaam for a year from the 1 September 1960: a useful holding-operation for which we were all properly grateful. There remained the question of accommodation, and both this and liaison-problems in general demanded some further intervention from home. Accordingly, in July 1959 the Secretary, accompanied again in part by the ever-helpful Gervase Mathew, once more went the round of the four Government Houses.

It should be said that, after a third incumbency, Sir Edward Twining had in 1958 relinquished the Governorship of Tanganyika and had been succeeded by Sir Richard Turnbull, previously Chief Secretary of Kenya. The Turnbulls, Dick and Beatrice, immediately became the firmest of friends, and Dar es Salaam, already the real basis of the Institute-enterprise, reflected their friendship. By this time the Bagamoyo scheme, faced by capital expenditure and above all, by distance from Dar where a full-blown university college was in the making, had faded from the foreground, and temporary lodgings were discovered in lieu within the metropolis. To them was shortly added, in accordance with the principle enunciated above (pp. 69 f.), a subsidiary centre at Kampala under the very active care of Dr. Merrick Posnansky, who had been Curator of the Uganda Museum and now became Assistant Director of the Institute.

In 1961 Neville Chittick assumed the Directorship, and, in addition to the responsibilities entailed in the general supervision of a number of students (British and African), undertook the now-classic excavation of sites on Kilwa Kisiwani (above, p. 68). But it was increasingly evident that geographically Dar was out on a limb, and some part of Chittick's early efforts, with those of others, was devoted to a quest for a more central headquarters and for closer integration with the component colleges of the new University of East Africa. This development was achieved, with the important incidental consequence that the University College of Nairobi made available, for a number of years and at a nominal rent, accommodation for the Institute's offices, library, and laboratory with certain privileges in respect of residence. The move from Dar es Salaam to Nairobi was completed by the end of 1964. Meanwhile Dr. Posnansky had taken up a lectureship at Makerere University College, and later went on to a Chair at Ghana University.

This is not the place in which to recall the active career of the Institute in any detail, but its success has been both undubitable and varied. The Kilwa excavations, which will constitute when fully published a cardinal document in East African archaeology, were used in progress as a vacation school for European and African students. In 1965 a generous grant from the Astor Foundation for three years financed a pilot study of Bantu origins and migrations, starting in the region of Lake Victoria and involving the co-operation of anthropologists and ethno-historians and of Americans, British, and Africans under the initial control of Dr. Brian Fagan on behalf of the Institute. In other directions, linguistic as well as historical, projects have been taken up by individuals or groups in the Institute's name, and an impressive periodical entitled *Azania* has come into being as a vehicle for new work. Those five laborious years were worth while; something new is at last coming out of Africa in a broad field of cultural studies, shared by Western and African scholars in happy and intelligent co-operation.

IX

EX ORIENTE LUX

Whilst the preliminaries of the African venture were still under way though already approaching port, another scheme of a partially comparable kind appeared a trifle unexpectedly upon the Academy's horizon. By way of preface let it be recalled that by the 'fifties the British Schools of Archaeology in Jerusalem and Iraq and the British Institute at Ankara formed a solid Asian extension of the earlier British foundations at Athens and Rome. But British enterprise had come to a halt at the western borders of Iran, a country where French scholarship had (with notable exceptions) long been without alien rival; whilst further east, in Afghanistan, the French had also enjoyed a near-monopoly of archaeological initiative under a Franco-Afghan treaty of 1922. Beyond Afghanistan, in the Indian subcontinent the British had of course dominated the scene politically and technologically, with increasing Indian participation, until Indo-Pakistan independence in 1947; but this situation was of an altogether different kind and scarcely comes into the present picture. At any rate, between Iraq and the Indian frontier there was a sizeable and historically important break in the continuity and orientation of British effort.

Let it not be thought that in all this there is any narrowing sense of national rivalry. The fact that, from Rome eastwards, British, French, German, and other schools, academies or institutes are liable to share the privileges of cultural intervention is nothing but advantageous, both mutually and to the host-country. Thereby varying skills and interests are brought to bear upon problems of varying kinds and facets, and incidentally material resources are multiplied. If there is emulation, it is of the healthy, stimulating kind proper to craftsmen working side by side in adjacent fields.

In the present instance the Perso-Afghan gap was, for British (and indeed for world) scholarship, a defect in the organic integrity of cultural research, of which many of us had long been conscious. When, therefore, in March 1959 a not widely known ex-member of the Persian Parliament, one who was also a publisher and a publicist, addressed a memorandum to the

British Council in London on Anglo-Iranian relations, the communication was received not without interest though perhaps with something rather like a wild surmise. It recalled that 'England has left the age of imperial domination behind. For the new era she needs fresh perspective. The extraordinary resourcefulness of the British mind and spirit will surely rise to these new demands. The writer, after a life-long and bitter opposition to British interference in Iranian affairs, is now a staunch supporter of close collaboration in all spheres and particularly in the cultural. . . .

'High ideals animate the British Council. But much more can be achieved in building a solid cultural edifice worthy of our two nations' traditions. Iran and England meet at many points. . . .'

Specifically, the writer had in mind the establishment of a counterpart of the Institut Français which occupied 'an imposing and spacious building, the largest of its kind in Teheran', but now needed reinforcement.

Mr. Majid Movaghar, for that was the name of this enlightened well-wisher, was not one who allowed unnecessary grass to grow. Before the end of that month he was in London, impressing his views in person upon 'the British Council, the Central Office of Information, the Information Office of the Duchy of Lancaster, the Foreign Office, the universities, and the British Museum, culminating' in correspondence with the Academy's Secretary who was abroad during this headlong crusade. The more he pursued the quest, Movaghar exclaimed, the greater the enthusiasm he met. On his return to Teheran, he would at once take up the question of a British Institute of Archaeology with the Shah and the Minister of Education. Not only that:

On my return the 'Mehr Cultural Foundation' will be created. I can assure you now that the Foundation would be very happy to be of any help in furthering the aims and objects of your Institute. In fact the two Institutions would be able to conduct their cultural activities to the mutual advantage. But again, as I have to register the Foundation and to perform the formalities before I can proffer any concrete suggestion, you, on behalf of your Government, would perhaps be gracious enough to put your Institute into operation, so as to substantiate your nation's interest in the project, before the Persian Government's liberal interest could be attracted to it. Looking forward to much fruitful co-operation . . .

In some fashion a little less clear this project was connected with the Moral Re-armament of the Nations which happened at the beginning of April 1959 to hold an assembly at Caux sur

Montreux in Switzerland. Word came that at this assembly, on his way back from London, Mr. Movaghar chaired an all-day Iranian session and read a message of encouragement from the Shah, 'after which the whole assembly stood while the International Chorus sang the Iranian National Anthem'. It was becoming manifest that, if born at all, the projected Institute would at least be born in the purple.

How serious was all this? During the following months the scheme for a British Institute in Iran continued intermittently to fill our ears and our post-bags, with an attachment of hopes and promises which, I am afraid, tended to diminish rather than increase our more phlegmatic English optimism. Moreover, the East African Institute, now at last, as related above, officially on its feet, required careful nursing, and there was little room in the cradle for a second child at the moment. However, Movaghar's urgent enthusiasm had not been in vain, and in Teheran he had a serious following. In particular, he and his friends had caught the constructive imagination of Mr. Charles Wilmot, who led the British Council's contingent in Iran and became a central figure in the early stages of the project. To him all gratitude is due. Towards the end of the year the London office of the Council— as we have seen, the original recipient of the scheme—took a hand, and the Academy's Secretary, now, after a third visit, released from the immediate pressures of East Africa, freely joined in with a good heart.

On the 1 December 1959 he had received a letter from Mr. Kenneth Johnstone, Deputy Director-General of the British Council:

> During this year I have been approached, as I think you have also, by a Persian gentleman named Majid Movaghar, who is interested in the possibility of setting up a British Institute of Iranian Studies in Teheran. I understand from him that he has also approached the Shah about the plan and has obtained a general blessing for it. I have consulted the Foreign Office who are prepared to take an interest in the proposal, although they cannot at this stage commit themselves to it. If, as I believe, you have also had some discussions with Mr. Movaghar, I should be grateful if you could spare me the time to talk the matter over with you since it concerns our Council directly and indirectly in a number of ways. . . .

That note opened a series of useful and exceedingly friendly conversations between Johnstone and the Secretary during the following twelve months. The paths to the Athenaeum and the Guards' Club were well and truly trodden, and much was done

or planned with a maximum of amicable hospitality and a minimum of writing—the way in which civilized business of importance is most intelligently transacted.

We began by discussing the personalia involved, and *in primis*
concluded that Movaghar's enthusiasm did in fact represent a
very genuine desire for progress, not only on his part but on that
of a number of influential backers in Teheran, perhaps including
the Shah himself. This enthusiasm, however, could not be expected to thrive on air; if (as we began to suspect) it was worth
following up, something must be done urgently to demonstrate
the seriousness of our own acceptance of the need for active
British participation in the cultural field of Iran.

At that point the Secretary offered a suggestion across the luncheon debris. If one thing was more certain than another, it was
the impossibility of steering a scheme for a full-blown Institute of
Persian (or Iranian) Studies through H.M. Treasury for 1960–1.
It was already too late to catch the 1960 Budget, and in any case
it was too soon after the East African episode (1959) to expect
Their Lordships to accept another overseas project of the kind.
The best that we could hope for was that useful device, a holding-
operation. On the spur of the moment a holding-operation
was devised, and Johnstone readily took it to his chiefs in first
instance.

The nature of the proposal is indicated by the letter dated
5 February 1960 in which Johnstone conveyed the British Council's favourable reaction:

> Following our telephone conversation earlier this week, I write to let
> you know that the Council would, in principle, be very willing to con-
> sider the offer which you so kindly made when we lunched together last
> December, to attach an archaeologist to the staff of the Council in Iran.
> If I am right, your proposal was that you would put into your own
> budget a sum at the rate of £2,000 per year which would represent the
> emoluments of the man concerned, and the Council would be respon-
> sible for providing him with an office and with reasonable space for
> storage of his material. . . .

The telephone conversation referred to was an attempt (as is
seen, successful) to bring the British Council's views to a head on
the eve of the February meeting of the Council of the Academy,
which as yet knew nothing about this plot. As always, the Academy's President, Sir Maurice Bowra, thought quickly and acted
decisively. (It is more than likely that he and the Secretary had
already discussed the project briefly in our usual staccato but
communicative fashion.) The Council of the Academy readily

concurred, and on the 11 February 1960 the Secretary was able to write formally to Johnstone as follows:

Our Council, in spite of the fact that its budget for 1960–61 was already pretty full, has decided that the opportunity of opening up Iran is not to be missed. It has accordingly welcomed what I may call the 'Attaché' scheme most warmly; and if David Stronach, the young Cambridge man of whom I spoke to you, reacts favourably, is prepared to pay him £1,000 p.a. for the year beginning on September 1st (or earlier, if possible) and also to make him a grant from one of our special funds towards the cost of his work in the field—making a total of about £1,500 in all. I have written today to Stronach in Baghdad to get his reactions to the principle of the thing. If the result of the year's trial is satisfactory we can build up, with Mr. Movaghar's help if possible, the nucleus of a reasonable working scheme.

For the moment, let me simply add this: that our Council warmly welcomed the possibility of co-operating with the British Council in this matter, and will do all it can to make the tentative operation a success.

So far, pretty good. But there still remained one man upon whom it was likely that the plan would win or fall: the David Stronach referred to in my letter to Johnstone. David, after leaving Cambridge, had worked on archaeological sites in Turkey and Iraq, and in 1958 he had been attracted somehow to my Charsada expedition on the North-west Frontier of Pakistan. There we worked industriously together for six or seven weeks on an important and complex site amongst Pathans and Afridis, and both I and his men learned to like his quiet and cheerful intelligence, whilst he succeeded in tolerating my critical impatience. In other words, he had passed the tests with honours, and now was the one man of my acquaintance with all the right qualities for the skilled and diplomatic job which awaited fulfilment in Teheran.

In the course of my letter to him on the 11 February, I wrote:

The plot is this: that for a year you shall be attached to the British Council in Iran as 'British Academy Attaché' beginning from September 1960 or earlier. . . . Your job will be, as apart from the fieldwork, to make all possible friendly contacts with the Iranian authorities, to advise any appropriate students that may come your way, and generally to warm up the nest for a larger project. . . .

Stronach at once threw alternative futures to the winds. By September he was happily installed with the British Council at Teheran, was acting in contact with all the relevant powers at the capital, and had plans for the continuation on an appreciable scale of an excavation previously initiated by him at Yarim Tepé in northern Iran. He was the perfect pioneer.

All this not merely kept the project of a British Institute alive
in Teheran but helped, as was intended, to accelerate it. Difficulties were not absent; they were to be accepted. For example
Movaghar's promise or anticipation that free quarters would be
provided for the proposed institute in Teheran dragged its feet
a little. But as against this the prospect of a State Visit of Queen
Elizabeth II and Prince Philip in March 1961 now put the
authorities into a particularly receptive mood, and the idea took
shape that the Visit would provide a suitably spectacular occasion for an official inauguration of a new British Institute housed
by Iranian generosity. At this stage H.E. the Minister of Court,
the late Hussain Ala, already apprised of the project, took an increasing interest in its progress, and had a strong ally in H.E. Dr.
Isa Sadiq, Minister of Education, who had recently been actively
sponsoring an E. G. Browne Memorial at Cambridge. The
Minister of Court, both in his own right and as having direct
access to the Shah, became a tower of strength to the enterprise;
if indeed 'tower' be the right synonym to apply to a very charming little old gentleman proud, above all, in having been at
Westminster School, of which he bravely wore a new Old Boy's
tie on every formal occasion. Under these happy auspices, and
with the British Royal Visit as a terminal date, decisive action
was now opportune and imperative.

I talked this over with Kenneth Johnstone who, through
Charles Wilmot, had his finger closely on the Persian pulse. At
the end of August 1960, the hard-working Movaghar had a particular house in view for the unborn Institute; but both this and
other matters, not least a more personal liaison with the interested Ministers and with Teheran University, now demanded
closer contact than London provided. Johnstone agreed: more
than that, it seemed to me that the moment had arrived to attack
with all guns. And both Maurice Bowra and I had been gunners.
We would open fire together.

With the backing of the Foreign Office, we set off on 11 December 1960. Sir Geoffrey Harrison and his colleagues welcomed
us with open arms in their remarkable mid-Victorian Embassy,
today, alas, devoid of the squadron of Indian lancers which our
lost Empire at one time provided for its adornment. The Ambassador and Wilmot had a busy programme ready for us. We
met and conferred with the Ministers, we were lunched and dined
by the University under its very helpful and understanding
Chancellor (or Rector) Dr. Ahmed Farhad, and we alternately
made and listened to suitably exuberant speeches. We struggled

6. Sir Maurice Bowra (President 1958–1962).

into morning-coats, as into ancient suits of armour, and waited upon H.I.M. the Shahanshah, who had been suitably briefed and very amiably and unreservedly blessed our enterprise. Thereafter a more leisurely conversation or Imperial monologue took us rapidly round the world in search of political virtue which (with a twinkle) was excessively hard to discover outside Iran: an entertaining and civilized half-hour. At the Embassy, Sir Geoffrey displayed hospitably for us the world of Teheran. We ended our week with a foray to Isfahan, still amongst the most lovely cities in the world.

It was an agreeable and useful episode. There was no doubt now as to the goodwill which would attend the consummation of our scheme in Teheran. The University would now quite definitely find housing for the Institute during its first two years. We had academic friends and friends at court. Only one trifling thing remained: to bring the Institute itself into being. H.M. Treasury held the trump card. Here neither Maurice Bowra nor the Secretary had by now any thought of failure. Nevertheless success, when it did come, came unexpectedly.

On 12 January 1961, not long after our return from Persia, a small crowd assembled in the room of the Financial Secretary, Sir Edward Boyle, at the Treasury building in George Street. At the head of the table sat Sir Edward, with Sir Ronald Harris, Third Secretary (who incidentally dealt with the Academy), beside him and a number of other Treasury folk here and there; on the other side sat the Duke of Devonshire, Professor Bryan Emery, and the Secretary of the Academy. The Duke of Devonshire was the President of a Committee set up by the Minister of Education to represent Britain in the UNESCO scheme for salving what could be salved of the antiquities which would be destroyed by the great reservoir about to drown 300 miles of the Nile Valley by the construction of the new Aswan High Dam. The Secretary of the Academy was present as Chairman of the Committee, and Bryan Emery was there as the principal archaeological executive. After argument which is not here relevant, the Financial Secretary decided to recommend a welcome grant of £20,000. The party was breaking up when some gadfly drove the Secretary of the Academy to corner Sir Edward about the Persian scheme and to indicate how much depended on an immediate government grant of £8,000 to enable the Institute to be formally established, primarily on its own merits but secondarily because of the forthcoming Royal Visit. Sir Edward grasped the situation and promptly said 'Yes'. The whole interchange lasted about five minutes.

This was of course unblushing opportunism. All sorts of angles had been cut and protocols violated. The only thing that could be said for it was that it worked. I apologized, however, immediately to Sir Ronald Harris who stood by and should have received the appeal in first instance, and later in my office I wrote to him a renewed apology and an explanation of the circumstances. For the record this letter should perhaps be quoted:

British Institute of Persian Studies in Teheran

First let me again apologise for my surprise packet at the end of our conversation with the Financial Secretary this afternoon. I had only just received confirmation of the offer of free premises from the University of Teheran and had not had time to forward the proposal through the proper channels. The element of urgency—the Queen's visit to Persia at the beginning of March—must be my excuse. It was all most improper.

For some considerable time members of the Persian Government and other influential Persians outside it have been representing to the British Council (as our cultural representative in Teheran) both the need for a British centre of Persian Studies and the Persian desire to facilitate the establishment of such an Institute. In particular, offers have been made of *free premises* if such an Institute could be established by the British Government. The existing Institute at Ankara, and others at Baghdad, Athens, Rome and elsewhere, were the general model, but it was hoped that the function of the Institute would extend widely into Persian culture, beyond, though of course including, history and archaeology.

Throughout these preliminary negotiations the British Council has been an encouraging intermediary, although not ultimately concerned in the development of the project. Recently the British Academy has been invited to send a delegation to Teheran to discuss the matter on the spot with all concerned. Accordingly in December 1960 Sir Maurice Bowra, President of the Academy, and I spent some time in Teheran and saw everyone from the Shah downwards. Our reception can only be described as enthusiastic, and there is no doubt that at the present time active British intervention in Persian cultural studies would be very warmly welcomed, incidentally as a replacement of the French participation which has hitherto been dominant but is now on the wane.

When we were in Teheran the proposal was discussed in detail with the Persian Minister of Education and with Dr. A. Farhad, Rector of Teheran University. They are both anxious that the new Institute shall be in some measure within the purlieus of the University. Suitable accommodation was indeed offered to us in the centre of the city; and that offer had just been confirmed by the Council of the University.

The general need for a centre for research in Persia as the watershed of early civilizations and as the home of much Asian art and literature in later times needs no emphasis. The pattern of British research and indeed of research generally is incomplete without a firm focus in that country. But there are now two special reasons for urgency in this matter: first the very practical enthusiasm on the part of the Persians to help—an enthusiasm which in an Eastern country cannot be guaranteed to last indefinitely!—and secondly their special anxiety to achieve something definite before the Queen's visit to Teheran on March 2nd. The University would very greatly appreciate the opportunity of placing in Her Majesty's hands some token indication that with their help this new Institute has in fact been inaugurated.

The approximate annual cost of such an Institute, on the basis of current costs in comparable institutions, is estimated at £8,000.

I am sorry that this letter has been so long but thought that you ought to know the facts fairly fully.

All was now well. Boyle sent this letter on to the Parliamentary Under-Secretary of the Foreign Office, Mr. J. B. Godber, M.P. The reply (23 January 1961—less than a fortnight after my first approach to the Financial Secretary!) was that

The project has our whole-hearted support. . . . From a political point of view, we regard the present as a particularly favourable moment at which to launch an enterprise of this kind. We believe that . . . the Iranians would welcome this British intervention. The project has the enthusiastic backing of the Shah, his Minister of Education and the Rector of the University of Teheran. It is significant that the idea of an Institute was first proposed by the Iranians, and their desire to see such a centre established is reflected in their offer of free premises. We are accordingly most anxious to take advantage of a gesture here which is unlikely to recur. The Royal visit to Teheran in March affords us a unique opportunity to derive the maximum goodwill from the proposal. . . .—In the light of the foregoing and of the contents of your letter, I hope i t will be possible to approve this at once. . . .

Events moved rapidly. At its meeting on 15 February 1961, the Council of the Academy appointed a Governing Council of the new Institute, with Professor (Sir) Max Mallowan as President and David Stronach as Director. Towards the end of the month the foundation of the Institute was announced in the House of Commons at question-time, and on 3 March Professor Mallowan was present at the University of Teheran when Dr. Farhad as Rector was thanked by Prince Philip for the University's hospitality to the Institute and the Queen also made a similarly graceful and gracious reference to this generosity in her speech.

Although not yet formally open, the Institute began on 16 October 1961 the first of three seasons of excavation at Pasargadae, the original capital of the Achaemenid dynasty. That this outstanding site was conceded to the Institute was itself a mark of special favour. Students began to arrive, and successful efforts were made to provide for them. In response to the vigorous campaigning of Professor Mallowan, as President of the Institute, the Wolfson Foundation liberally provided £10,000 for the purpose of establishing studentships during the Institute's first quinquennium, and Iranian Oil Participants Limited added a further annual £2,000 to be followed later by a generous grant of £5,000 from the Calouste Gulbenkian Foundation for the purchase of books. The time had come to hang out the flags. It was in fact as an establishment already busily at work that the 'British Institute of Persian Studies' was ceremoniously opened on 10 and 11 December 1961. At the Inaugural Meeting on the 11th, Dr. Ahmad Farhad, Rector of the University, presided over a large and distinguished audience of Iranian and British guests, and, following a reception, Sir Maurice Bowra, as President of the British Academy and one of the two 'Founding Fathers' of the Institute, delivered an address on Edward Fitzgerald. It was received with acclamation. Speeches were delivered by Dr. Farhad, Mr. Hussain Ala, and Professor Mallowan, and the whole function was a friendly and auspicious triumph. The auspices have continued to be friendly and are likely to remain so, for the Institute has developed into a cultural embassy of high standing and has become a part of the Persian scene.

Reference has been made to the beginning of the Pasargadae excavations, in full swing even before the formal opening. But from the outset it was emphasized that, unlike most other British institutions of the kind, the new Institute would not confine its official energies to art and archaeology, but would 'endeavour to provide facilities for the study of Persian civilization in all its length and breadth, from the remote past to present times, in many aspects, in different disciplines'. As evidence of intent, one of the Institute's earliest publications was a recent study by Professor A. J. Arberry of an early Persian epic, the *Humāy-nāma*, as the first of a series of Persian texts; and in the second volume of the Institute's annual periodical *IRAN* (1964) the same author printed three Persian poems as an exposition of 'some of the qualities which make for great poetry in Persian'. Professor Arberry's premature death in 1969 was a great loss to Persian studies and to the Institute which professed and professes them.

X

THE ONE THAT FAILED

IN 1947 the Scarbrough Report, reviewing certain of the cultural gaps in the post-war world, strongly urged the need for a new balance between classical and oriental studies, and in particular advocated the establishment of a research institute in the Far East, preferably in Peking. Unhappily this proposal, though included by H.M. Government within its general acceptance of the Report, was not immediately carried into effect. Whether in fact, had the scheme materialized at the time, it could in any viable form have survived subsequent political events may be more than doubted. Anyway the opportunity, such as it was, passed without action.

But the idea took root. In 1951 a growing realization of the need, from academic and wider standpoints, for just such a liaison between West and East induced the Universities of Oxford, Cambridge, and London to set up an Inter-University Committee to explore the possibilities outlined in the Report. The Committee met on a number of occasions between 1951 and 1958 but seems to have achieved little of practical consequence, admittedly under changing and increasingly complex circumstances. Eventually it limped into the Secretary's room at the British Academy.

Administratively the moment was not a happy one. As recounted above, the Academy was already involved in the undeniable need for action of some sort in East Africa; it was shortly to be concerned, also with a certain sense of urgency, in important developments in Iran; and at the end of both these turnpikes the toll-gate of H.M. Treasury lay menacingly across the road. With the advent of yet a third scheme, congestion threatened.

Nevertheless, it was sufficiently clear to all of us that the Far Eastern proposal could not be turned abruptly into the hedgerows. The high desirability of a British research-centre in the Far East was beyond dispute. The question was primarily one of (a) location and (b) ways and means. At its meeting on 15 January 1959, the Academy's Section IV (Oriental Studies) approved a plan for a Far Eastern Institute in Tokyo, financed by the Government but sponsored by the Academy. And on 18 March 1959 the whole project was reviewed by the Academy's Council in conjunction with members of the Inter-University Committee and representatives of the Cultural Relations Department of H.M. Foreign Office.

At this meeting a number of points were discussed in a preliminary fashion, and the following provisional decisions emerged:

  (i) The location of the School or Institute: whilst Peking remained the obvious centre, present political conditions were thought to be unsuitable, and the only feasible alternative appeared to be Tokyo.

 (ii) Finance should make provision for a staff comprising at the top a Director and an Assistant Director, with something like six adequate studentships. The Director should be a scholar of some eminence, able to carry weight with Japanese and other Eastern scholars and equal in prestige to those of other European countries stationed in Japan.

(iii) Subject to Treasury approval, the Academy would be prepared to include the proposed Institute in its triennial budget, alongside the routine demands for established schools and institutes in other parts of the world.

 (iv) Meanwhile it was decided to assemble a small Committee representing the Inter-University Committee, the Council of the Academy, and H.M. Foreign Office; and that this Committee should hold its first meeting on 29 April 1959.

At this meeting, held under the chairmanship of Sir Maurice Bowra, President of the Academy, the need for a Far Eastern Institute was re-affirmed for three main functions: for assisting British scholars embarking on or engaged in Eastern studies, for maintaining a supply of Englishmen with a thorough knowledge of Eastern languages, and for ensuring British prestige vis-à-vis other national (e.g. French and German) institutes in the East. Questions of staff, accommodation, and capital and running costs were considered in detail, and the project began to assume something like a tangible shape.

At this point an ineluctable break occurred in the development of the scheme for a reason already indicated: the presence of two comparable and therefore rival projects in the pipe-line. In 1959 the British Institute of History and Archaeology in East Africa came into being, and was followed early in 1961 by the new Institute of Persian Studies at Teheran. That was good going, but the pace could not be sustained. To approach the Treasury yet again, until a decent interval had elapsed, would have been to court certain failure and would have been a psychological blunder of the first order. It would have imperilled the whole balance of confidence which had now been firmly established in Academy–Treasury relationships.

But by 1962 it was time for the sun to rise again in the East, however misty the horizon. Both the Foreign Office and the old Inter-University Committee expressed a renewal of their interest in the project; and at its February meeting the Council of the Academy instructed the Committee appointed in 1959 to reassemble and to proceed with the proposal for a Far Eastern Institute. At the same time there was a strong feeling that there should be some re-thinking of the question of location, once more with a bias towards Peking rather than Tokyo. The President (Sir Maurice Bowra) undertook to explore the possibilities with the Ambassador of the People's Republic of China. In due course he and the Secretary had conversations with the Chinese Chargé d'Affaires. With perfect courtesy the matter was referred to Peking. Always with perfect courtesy, nothing happened. We were back in Tokyo. Incidentally, through various responsible channels it became known to us that the establishment of a British Institute would be warmly welcomed there. An official colouring had already been given to these reports by the Anglo-Japanese Mixed Commission, set up to deal with mutual interests between the two countries, which on 30 October 1962 gave its formal blessing to the scheme.

At the same time (September 1962) a new factor added its weight to the Tokyo proposal. Word came to the Academy that an influential member of the British diplomatic staff in Tokyo had been able to interest a personal friend, a wealthy Australian businessman with commercial interests in Japan, in the project, and as a result the 'anonymous donor' (as he is known throughout the files) promised to support the scheme once it was definitely under way. No precise sum was mentioned, but it was expected to be a generous one (something like £60,000 was later rumoured). It was strongly suspected that the benefaction would be available only if the Institute were located in Japan.

By now certain aspects of the scheme were becoming clearer whilst others developed new complexities. Negotiation between an increasing number of interested parties outside the control of the Academy dragged on into 1964. The potential donor insisted that he would not commit himself to any sum until he was assured that H.M. Government were backing the project and a financial statement was laid before him making it clear that with his contribution the Institute would become a reality. The Treasury was, not unnaturally, loath to commit itself to a theoretical scheme which itself, on the other hand, could not become practicable without a Treasury guarantee. Not least, a new and vital element was introduced in an attempt to solve the key-problem of accommodation in Tokyo: an element which involved the Foreign Office in a fresh context, together with the British Council and the Ministry of Public Building and Works. The scene was rapidly overcrowding.

In a discussion of priorities at a meeting of the British Institute of Far Eastern Studies Committee on 5 June 1964, it was decided that a necessary preliminary to any attempt to sort out the tangle was a determined approach to H.M. Treasury with a view to securing an expression of Government approval at least in principle. Conscious that the base for such an attack was not, in Treasury terms, a particularly strong one, Lord Robbins, as President of the Academy, with the Secretary undertook to make the attempt. In July 1964 the little delegation went into battle in Treasury Chambers and, in all the circumstances, made what I think may be described as a good showing. The formal reply from a Third Secretary, dated 27 July, went as far as a cautious Treasury could be expected to go more than six months ahead of the next budget. As a record and as a skilfully courteous piece of Treasury composition, here it is:

Dear Sir Mortimer,

We discussed recently the proposal made by Lord Robbins and yourself to include in the grant application of the British Academy for the triennium which begins next April [1965] provision for the running costs of a new British Institute of Far East Studies in Tokyo.

It is, as you know, extremely difficult for us to give assurances about the amounts to be provided in next year's Estimates at this stage, and it is particularly difficult for us to comment on one item in your future grant application before you have been able to submit the application as a whole. However, you were able to assure us that this was the only new Institute for which you would be seeking Exchequer help in the new triennium. We can tell you that we would be prepared to recommend it sympathetically to Ministers, provided, as we understood to be the case, there were no other proposals at the time from the Academy for substantial additional sums of Exchequer money. You will appreciate that this letter refers to the running costs of the proposed new Institute and not at all to capital costs.

Yours sincerely,
W. W. Morton.

How far that friendly response would be acceptable to the 'anonymous donor' remained to be seen, but on the whole it was not devoid of comfort to the promoters. Incidentally, this was the last occasion on which the name 'Institute of Far East(ern) Studies' was applied officially to the project. On diplomatic advice from Tokyo the style and title were henceforth changed to 'Institute of East Asian Studies' as likely to be more welcome in Japan—presumably as implying a less other-worldly remoteness.

After the Treasury, the next priority confronting the Academy Committee was that of accommodation. Here a new factor had arisen which simultaneously complicated the whole problem and held out new hope. Information had percolated through from the Foreign Office and from the British Council direct that there was a proposal afoot to build new offices for the British Council in Tokyo upon land hitherto occupied by decayed buildings attached to the British Embassy; and a further suggestion had gathered growing support that provision for the proposed Institute might be included in the new Council building, if suitable arrangements could be agreed by the Council and by the Ministry of Public Building and Works. It was further reported (June 1964) that the 'anonymous donor' had 'liked the idea that the proposed Institute should be in close contact with the British Council in Tokyo and was not at all alarmed at the figure of £60,000' which had been put to him tentatively as a contribution to the capital cost.

Along these lines, almost neck and neck with our approach to the Treasury, things began to move. Both the British Council and the Academy began to draw up detailed schedules of accommodation required, and the Ministry of Public Building and Works got down to its own considerable side of the operation. Details need not concern us here, but in broad outlines it was agreed that the Institute would require the equivalent of two floors of the new building, one of a residential kind and one for administration. The essential library of the Institute could be combined with that of the Council, with the addition of a room or alcove for specialist books. In October 1965 a meeting was held at the Foreign Office to conflate these various details and to look forward. The latter operation was inevitably hedged round by the extent and speed of the co-operation of the Treasury and the M.O.P.B. & W. but it was estimated that the Academy's requirements might cost about £45,000 or, with provision for furniture and equipment, about £60,000, the sum already provisionally agreed, as it seems, by the 'anonymous donor'. All appeared to be going well, save that a definite high-level guarantee was still needed to enable the Academy to collect the anonymous benefaction which had now been waiting for several years and obviously could not wait much longer.

At this time (1965), as though to complicate an already sufficiently complex situation, the British Academy, like the Royal Society, was removed from direct contact with H.M. Treasury and placed under the Department of Education and Science as our future intermediary with the sources of wealth and power. The change-over might have been disastrous, but happily the Academy came within the purview of Mr. T. R. Weaver, Deputy Secretary of D.E. & S., and our problems were received with ready understanding. Negotiations proceeded without perceptible interruption.

The final climax came on 13 September 1967. On that day a meeting of representatives of the Ministry of Public Building and Works, the British Council, the Foreign Office, and the British Academy (the Secretary) assembled at the M.O.P.B. & W. to finalize the over-all scheme of the new British Council-cum-Institute building in respect of space and cost (in as far as Tokyo prices were available). The square-footage of the share proposed for the Institute was 4,000 and its approximate cost would be £55,000, including Departmental Expenses, for the building-cost, plus £10,000 for furniture, etc., making a total of £65,000. This total tallied closely with previous estimates. The position of the now almost legendary 'anonymous donor' was still unresolved, but at the end of the meeting it was felt that at last, even though the capital outlay might have to be sought elsewhere, the whole scheme was approaching viability. Time was still, as it appeared, on our side since no money would be required for capital expenditure until 1971.

But in fact time was not on our side. Came the financial crisis of 1967–8 and the abrupt halt to all new enterprises. On 11 January 1968, the following letter from the Director-General of the British Council to the Secretary of the Academy settled the whole business for the time-being:

Dear Rik,

I am afraid that I have some unwelcome news to give you about the proposed new building in Tokyo which we hoped would house both the British Council and the proposed Institute of Far Eastern Studies. A few months ago it seemed possible that at last we were going to get the money to build and we therefore began to prepare plans with the Ministry of Public Building and Works. However, the devaluation crisis has now intervened, and, although we hope to emerge pretty well in regard to recurrent expenditure, we have had to take a sizeable cut in the provision for our capital programme. We have therefore decided to look into the question of renting rather than building.

We are naturally disappointed at this development, but I think you will not be surprised in the prevailing situation. . . .

Yours ever,
Paul Sinker.

A sad little story. A scheme untimely born and as it would seem untimely dead. There were too many doctors at its bedside. We may now, with a proper impatience, await its resurrection.

XI

RESEARCH PROJECTS

By the middle 'sixties the Academy was gradually approaching an income-level at which its impact on research could begin to extend beyond a restricted charity into fields of new and autonomous enterprise. In other words it could now, within widening limits, not merely approve and encourage with mild support but could at last, as is its proper destiny, contrive and lead. Accordingly the Academy's President, Lord Robbins, invited Sections at their meetings in January 1966 to consider the formulation of research-schemes of a major character worthy of initiation and maintenance as specifically Academy enterprises.

In the event the Council and its Research Fund Committee have found themselves confronted by a number of proposals which fall roughly into two categories: those schemes which have sprung Athene-like from the brain of the Academy, and those other more alien projects which are of such manifest merit as to claim inclusion and nurture within the family-circle. It may be that one or two of them were even discovered in baskets on the doorstep, but no matter. In all instances they are regarded as possessing some special claim to scholarly, administrative, and financial aid from the Academy and are distinct from those lesser or less ambitious breeds whose fate is to scramble adventitiously for what is left. The committees controlling the two main categories are Committees of the Academy.

Within the first category ranks *in primis* the investigation into the *Early History of Agriculture*, which has been from the outset an Academy project of the highest importance to our understanding of the human achievement in economic and social terms. On the borderline of the first and second category is the *Medieval Latin Dictionary* which began as an international enterprise but, in the more limited context of the British Isles, has always been, with varying industry though on the whole with increasing drive, the prerogative of the Academy. So also has been the British section of the international effort to produce a *Corpus of Medieval Stained Glass*. On the other hand three schemes—those for the publication of a *Sylloge of Coins of the British Isles* and of a collection of *Early English Church Music*, and the maintenance of a Computer

Librarian—were, like the *Early History of Agriculture*, initiated by the Academy; whilst two others—the systematic publication of the *Oxyrhynchus Papyri* and of the vast accumulation of the *Works and Correspondence of Jeremy Bentham*—have leaned increasingly upon the Academy's support. The most recent candidate for full Academy patronage has been the *English Place-name Society* which had from its outset been supported partially by the Academy but had in effect been fathered by University College, London.

The original intention in 1966 was to classify accepted proposals into two grades: Major Research Projects, and the rest. The growth in the number of applications has tended to render classification of this sort invidious or impossible. Certain of the schemes, involving permanent staffs, have obviously in practice a more exacting claim upon the Academy's resources than have others which depend mainly upon the more casual part-time services of individual scholars: in that sense the *Early History of Agriculture*, the *Medieval Latin Dictionary*, and the *Medieval Stained Glass*, to take examples, have some special claim to financial continuity. But in most instances the ultimate arbiters must continue to be successful progress and the availability of funds.

In the following pages notes are added on the development of these various undertakings down to 1969.

(i) THE EARLY HISTORY OF AGRICULTURE

One of the first to respond to Lord Robbins's invitation in 1966 was Section X (Archaeology), and the prime inspirer was Professor Grahame Clark. Just before the Sectional meetings, Clark wrote to the Secretary: 'I would like to propose that Section X sponsors a project to investigate "The early history of Agriculture; its origins, spread and development in the Old World". To be successful, such a project needs the active support of natural scientists—ideally under a man like Sir Joseph Hutchinson, F.R.S. [Drapers' Professor of Agriculture at Cambridge] and I would hope it might be possible to engage the interest of the Royal Society. . . . My feeling is that a project sponsored by the two bodies would attract outside funds. I could visualise work being done at existing centres. Funds would be needed for hiring young research workers, preferably post-doctoral, and providing for travel, attendance at excavations and so on. . . .'

The proposal was warmly and widely welcomed. After all it required no very specialized thinking to recognize in the invention and exploitation of food-production Man's greatest achievement, if not in all time at least between the lighting of the first fire and the splitting of the first atom. The meeting of Section X on 6 January 1966 invited Professor Clark to draw up a memorandum on his scheme, with special reference to Problems and Machinery. 'It was envisaged that a sub-committee would eventually be formed and it was hoped that this would be in part composed of Fellows of the Royal Society in addition to Fellows of the British Academy.'

The Academy's Research Committee and Council fell into line, and a 'British Academy Committee on the Early History of Agriculture' was promptly established, consisting of Professor J. G. D. Clark, F.B.A., Professor H. Godwin, F.R.S., Professor C. F. C. Hawkes, F.B.A., Professor Sir Joseph Hutchinson, C.M.G., F.R.S., Professor E. M. Jope, F.B.A., and Professor Stuart Piggott, F.B.A. At its first meeting, held at Peterhouse, Cambridge, on 23 April 1966, Sir Joseph Hutchinson was elected Chairman. It was also agreed in principle to set up the Research Project at Cambridge where a number of research-centres in cognate fields would be available for consultation and collaboration: for instance, the Sub-Department of Quaternary Research under Professor Godwin, the Department of Agriculture under Sir Joseph Hutchinson, the Agriculture Research Council's Institute of Animal Physiology, the National Institute of Agricultural Botany, and of course the Department of Archaeology and Anthropology. In anticipation it may here be recorded that with gratifying speed the University authorities consented to the setting up of this new Project in the Department of Archaeology and Anthropology, and to making the services of the Director and the necessary accommodation available at no cost to the scheme. Not least, Mr. E. S. Higgs, Senior Assistant in Research in the Department of Archaeology and Anthropology, was appointed Director of the Project.

Now as to the scheme itself. Its definition and orientation were largely the work of Grahame Clark, and in what follows much will be derived from the successive memoranda which he prepared for the Cambridge Committee and the various committees of the Academy.

The central purpose of the Project is to examine and trace the development of the earliest agricultural economy in Europe. The principal fields of research include:

(a) Ecological studies, including the history of physiographic, climatic, and vegetational change since the end of the Ice Age in the several territories concerned.

(b) Biological data from archaeological sites, including animal bones and remains of crops.

(c) Settlement pattern and material equipment relating to early farming communities.

(d) Historical sources.

(e) Recent farming practice.

On this, the barest forecast of the scope of the Project, it was clear that the whole enterprise would be frustrate without an appreciable staff and equipment from the outset, within the framework liberally provided by the University of Cambridge. A budget, carefully and even meticulously itemized for the first five years (beginning in 1967–8), was presented to the Academy, which allotted £5,000 from its Research Fund for the first year and has repeated the allotment annually. A first charge on this grant was the provision of two Research Fellows, to whom a third was added by the Wenner-Gren Foundation of New York. Thereafter, Mr. Higgs was able to deploy a small but effective force, with invaluable subsidiary help from a number of interested scholars.

It was planned in first instance to focus attention on Greece as a bridgehead into Europe, with the study of the economy of Palaeolithic man as a basis for further research. (It was astonishing to find, on critical examination, how little detailed and scholarly work had been done upon this basic study.) Material for this was beginning to become available from sites excavated by Higgs and others (with Academy and other aid) during 1961–7 in Epirus, notably at the caves of Asprochaliko and Kastritsa which between them had provided a complete sequence from before 40000 B.C. to later than 9000 B.C. (Incidentally, Mr. Higgs was awarded the Rivers Memorial Medal of the Royal Anthropological Institute for this work.) In the task of assessing the physiographic background of human settlement in Epirus, the team had the advantage of close association with Dr. C. Vita-Finzi and Dr. D. R. Harris of University College, London, and of Dr. W. van Zeist of Groningen whose pollen-analytical work extends as far east as Thrace. Sir Joseph Hutchinson, with aid from the Royal Society, also spent some weeks in Epirus in 1967 investigating the relationships between the human exploitation of the region and erosional processes.

Meanwhile the three Research Fellows, who had assumed their appointments in October 1967, had taken up their allotted tasks in various problems and places. Mr. M. R. Jarman (a triple-first graduate in Archaeology at Cambridge) began by spending six weeks as Wenner-Gren Fellow at Mrs. David Oates's excavations at Choga Mami in northern Iraq, where, in addition to work on animal bones, he established a system for recovering floral remains from deposits by flotation; over 5,000 specimens were collected. He also organized and began the study of faunal remains from Neolithic Knossos, with a view to the interpretation of this analysis and its relevance to the domestication of cattle in the Near East.

At the same time Mr. S. Payne (a Cambridge graduate with qualifications in the Natural Sciences and Archaeology) was engaged as one of the British Academy Fellows upon the study of sheep and goats in prehistory, and was engaged upon basic methods relevant to the analyses of assemblages from archaeological sites. The other Academy Fellow, Miss B. Field (a Botany graduate from University College, London) was studying the first batch of botanical material from Iraq.

In one way and another this first year's work (1967–8) was inevitably exploratory and tentative in character. Good progress, however, had been made in defining problems, in assessing the most likely opportunities for intensive field-work, and in refining procedures. Initial interest had been focussed on livestock, largely reserving plant-husbandry to the next phase. Meanwhile the project demanded a mingling of hard work with patience.

To define results more narrowly, during the summer of 1968 Mr. Jarman followed his work in Iraq by taking samples and making metrical analyses of available skeletal material representing a period of 20,000 years to the present day in Epirus and Crete. He obtained sufficient data relevant to changes in the morphology of the domesticated animals to provide for several years of statistical analysis by himself and future research-workers. Such comprehensive data were not available elsewhere in Europe, and should for the first time provide an adequate platform from which to develop these studies both in Europe and in the Near East. To complement Jarman's results, Mr. Payne had worked with promising results in the Peloponnese and in Thrace.

Crete has been mentioned: an island offering special opportunity from the apparent fact that it was not occupied by the prototypes of the domestic animals. The introduction of these is therefore likely to have been by Neolithic farmers and thus to present in some measure an isolated problem. The change in various features (in biotype, erosion, etc.) may be expected to differ from those of the mainland and to provide useful comparative data. During the year, in collaboration with Dr. Vita-Finzi, Mr. Jarman began to work on the beginning of prehistoric farming in the island.

In the spirit of reconnaissance, Dr. Vita-Finzi also joined Mr. Higgs in the location of archaeological sites and territories in Israel, particularly in their relationship to the physiography of the region and to present-day agricultural exploitation. Israel is not only a particularly suitable area for testing hypotheses but within readily workable compass also possesses an extensive, recent, and accessible literature on climate and environment, much of it relating appropriately to subsistence agriculture.

Another region where preliminary investigation showed promising possibilities was Turkey, where Mr. David French, who had excavated there for many years and was shortly to become Director of the British Institute of Archaeology at Ankara, was particularly co-operative.

During 1968-9 attention has been concentrated upon (1) methods of sampling animal and plant remains, (2) the techniques of analysing samples, and (3) the interpretation of biological materials from archaeological sites in terms of the utilization of environment. This has involved respectively field-trials at excavation sites, laboratory work, and the assessment of individual sites and of their environments in terms of their potential for occupation and subsistence. Good co-operation was secured from directors of numerous excavations, and financial help for field-expenses was received from the Faculty of Classics at Cambridge and the Crowther Beynon Fund administered by the Museum of Archaeology and Ethnology there.

The task of collecting and analysis both of plant and of animal remains continued on sites in northern Greece and Epirus, and again at Knossos in Crete. Work was also resumed in Israel in association with the Israel Museum and in Turkey with the Ankara Institute. At the same time it was proposed, at the invitation of the British School at Rome, to extend to southern Italy where the School is at present active.

In one way and another the Project is busily improving methods and collecting data which, in bulk and quality, are beginning to form an impressive and substantially new body of evidence on man's economy, enterprise, and environment. The path is inevitably a long one and speedy conclusions of determinate value are not to be expected. No doubt from time to time—perhaps every two or three years—an attempt may usefully be made to marshal the evidence so far and to discern possibly some hint as to the way in which it is moving. But it is both likely and proper that for some time to come the results of individual enquiries under the Project will continue to form fodder for periodical interim reports rather than for rounded conclusions. After all, for how many years was the *Origin of Species* in the making? And here, in the *Early History of Agriculture*, we are concerned with nothing less than the primary origins and prerequisites of civilization!

(ii) THE MAKING OF A DICTIONARY

The fabrication of dictionaries is a traditional and congenial occupation of academies. There is no marvel in this fact; the business is at the same time an exercise in exact scholarship and a bloodless, timeless sport, perhaps enhanced by its appeal to that familiar human trait, the urge to collect. Yes, 'timeless' is the epithet. Save for the devoted few, it is essentially a part-time employment. The present chapter is about to recall a project of this kind whereof the organizing committee might for a whole year, nay two years, lapse into recess. The theme is largely a Word-List whose Editor, after years and agonies of labour, in 1954 'expects to have it ready for the printer by the end of 1956. It will probably take another year to get it through the press and ready for publication'. In the event it reached the light on 24 June 1965. The delay was not the Editor's and in any case will not matter for ever, but even from this extending reach of time I find it difficult not to 'sound my barbaric yawp' a trifle harshly at the recollection. Less barbarously, others have done so before me. And then there is the sequel, the Dictionary itself.

But first the beginning. Around the middle of the seventeenth century the great Charles Du Cange compiled his monumental dictionary of medieval Latin, *Glossarium ad Scriptores Mediae et Infimae Latinitatis* which with minor scholarly attention remained the standard work in the field for more than two and a half centuries. Indeed, pending the publication of its modern successor it still (1969) substantially retains its premier status. Already, however, well inside the nineteenth century there was a movement afoot to replace it wholly or in part by a new Dictionary of Medieval Latin, and the publishing house of John Murray put a considerable sum of money into a scheme for an abridged version of

Du Cange for the use of English students: a scheme which proved
too ambitious from both the human and the financial standpoints
and had to be abandoned in 1882. An attempt to revive it in 1897
similarly failed, but in 1913 at the Historical Congress in London
a considered proposal was brought forward by Mr. R. J. White-
well for a Dictionary of Medieval Latin on historical principles
comparable with those which had governed another Murray's
Oxford English Dictionary.

The Great War cut across the development of this proposal but
in 1920 it was revived as a new Du Cange by the recently founded
Union Académique Internationale, which seemed to be the
natural home for an international project of this dimension. The
Commission, however, nominated by the Union to examine
the proposal reported against a universal *Thesaurus* or *Novum Glossarium Linguae Latinae Medii Aevi* on the grounds that this would be
too vast an enterprise for the powers and finances of the U.A.I.
Instead it advocated a limited programme restricted roughly to
the Merovingian and Carolingian periods, i.e. between *c.* A.D. 500
and the eleventh century; the terminal date to be determined
nationally or regionally, e.g. for France 967, for England 1066.
The chief administrative instrument would be a Dictionary Committee centred upon Paris. A *Bulletin* would be published from
time to time to keep contributors in touch with progress. A Director of the Dictionary and eventually a Secretary-General would
be appointed to control the operation. Questions of type and format would have to be decided. And there were other problems,
not all of them easy of solution. For example, 'What should be
done about the texts of non-participant countries?' 'How should
the work be divided amongst the different countries?' More formidable still, 'What should be done about countries which did
not possess ancient Latin texts?' And 'What about foreign words
which had not been Latinized?' The cynic might already have
begun to sense a slight *tremblement* in this new tower of good intent.
The basic limitation of the over-all project to the Early Middle
Ages was enough in itself to start potential schisms. The independently minded Rumanians, originally keen to collaborate,
threatened to strike if the twelfth to sixteenth centuries were left
out in the cold, and the British were at least implicitly impatient
of a Domesday barrier.

Eventually the whole of this unreal *mélange* broke down more
or less happily for working purposes into its component parts:
that is into national projects wherever the spirit was willing,
notably but not exclusively in Britain and Germany. For Britain

the British Academy in 1924 appointed two Committees, one to collect British and Irish material for the international Glossarium at Paris (limited as has been said to the sixth to eleventh or twelfth centuries), which began to appear tentatively in 1957 under the editorship of Professor Franz Blatt of Aarhus, and another to do the same for a dictionary of later Latin in Britain and Ireland (about 1086, Domesday Book, to about 1550). These two Committees were amalgamated in 1931, when the original dichotomy had lost any validity that it may have had and it was evident that the only viable British scheme would envisage a new and comprehensive Medieval Dictionary of the Latin used in the British Isles from the sixth to the sixteenth centuries. It should be recorded also that the work for the British Isles was aided substantially by a Scottish Committee established in 1926 under the Secretaryship of Dr. W. R. Cunningham; by an Irish Committee under the Secretaryship originally of Professor O'Meara and later of Dr. L. Bieler; and by committees formed in the United States to recruit contributors and to prepare lists of authorities.

Gradually the lists and slips began to accumulate, unostentatiously and with gaps particularly in technical, theological, and philosophical texts. Before the end of the first decade it was abundantly clear that some sort of interim action was needed to stimulate interest, attract new volunteers, and provide a nuclear pattern of procedure. It was decided to publish a List of all the Latin words which had been collected by the Medieval Latin Dictionary Committee before the end of 1932. Every word in this collection would now be noted for all to see, together with the earliest and latest date and some indication of meaning. The material would fall into two groups, one (pre-Conquest) fairly complete, the other (post-Conquest) still slowly a-building. Naturally the *apparatus* comprised no more than a choice from the data available.

The *Medieval Latin Word-List from British and Irish Sources*, prepared by J. H. Baxter and Charles Johnson, was accordingly published by the Oxford University Press for the British Academy in 1934, in terms of time a creditable achievement and in terms of sales and reputation an instant, perhaps surprising success. Within the following twenty years (which after all included a World War) it was reissued no less than five times. It is in intent an incomplete anticipatory index, not a treatise, but its slim text is full of savour. It has about it the good smell of the kitchen and, if the full meal, the Dictionary, was still afar off, here was a rough *vinum Anglicanum* (with little enough of the Falernian in its memory) to wash down the waiting.

As the *Word-List* (1934, etc.) poured gently but persistently from the press, question arose as to its continuing adequacy and, in particular, whether to prepare a Supplementary List or to go all out for a new and up-to-date edition. Increasing conviction that the Dictionary itself was not yet to be of this bad world favoured the more comprehensive alternative, and in 1965 the *Revised Medieval Latin Word-List*, prepared by R. E. Latham on the lines of its predecessors, was issued by the same publishers. It was based upon something like half a million slips, and was designed to serve as a guide to a body of writings

immensely greater in bulk than the whole extant corpus of Classical Latin and incomparably less investigated and digested. . . . The Latin language in the British Isles, as elsewhere in Western Europe, continued for over a thousand years to enrich its means of expression in order to meet the varying needs of an ever-changing society. . . . From the 12th to the 15th century, while scholars wrote for an international public in a Latin that scarcely betrays their British background . . ., the prac-titioners of the common law developed a host of *vocabula artis* that can have meant nothing to a Continental lawyer, and the clerks who drew up manorial accounts and court rolls did not scruple to latinize terms employed by local peasants, fishermen, and craftsmen that were quite possibly unintelligible in the next parish.

Perhaps after all the international *Glossarium* had been wise to curb its curiosity after the eleventh century!

On the title-page of the *Revised Word-List* the operative word was 'Latham'. Through the years the combined scholarly and ad-ministrative task of propelling the Dictionary along its devious course had gradually exceeded even the herculean powers of a Charles or H. C. Johnson, to both of whom the project had owed more than can be told. By 1947 it had become essential to find an assistant capable of preparing the Supplementary Word-List, which subsequently grew into the *Revised Word-List*. In the post-War years (as indeed long before them) money for such luxuries was hard to come by, but in July 1947 the Medieval Latin Dictionary Committee invited Mr. R. E. Latham, who had for many years been a considerable contributor to the Dictionary and was now an Assistant Keeper of the Public Records, to under-take the job. Mr. Latham accepted the invitation and hoped to be able to devote ten hours a week to the work; for which the Com-mittee offered him the 'minimum salary of £200 yearly'. It was expected that he would complete his task in two years!

This raises the question of the Committee's finances. Until the advent of Mr. Latham the whole project had been conducted in the economic environment of a past or passing age: it was founded upon voluntary and honorary effort. In an earlier chapter it has been recalled that the Academy's total income at this time was little more than negligible, and it is in the circumstances scarcely surprising that the annual grant to the Dictionary for 1947 and for nine years afterwards remained at a level £300. Attempts to elicit aid from elsewhere seem to have been received with little sympathy by a preoccupied world. Gradually, as year followed year of plodding, this lack of sympathy began to spread to the Academy itself. Although the Academy's annual Treasury grant was slowly increasing, so were the demands of the dependant Schools and other claimants. The pressure became perceptible in 1957, and in that year the grant to the Dictionary was reduced to £250. In March 1958, the Academy's Section II (Medieval and Modern History) reviewed the situation and its Chairman wrote to the Chairman of the Dictionary Committee:

Last year I remember there was some hesitation on the part of the Section regarding renewal of the grant of £250 to the Medieval Latin Dictionary. The Section felt that they would like to know how much longer there would be need for an annual grant of this kind. As the matter is coming up again in a few weeks could you possibly give me any light on the subject? The Section, I know, would probably be more generous if they felt that this were really the last occasion for a grant.

'How much longer?' forsooth! Looking back upon the scene it is not difficult to review it very much as the Academy's Secretary remembers appraising it at the time. A vast and complex work of scholarship had been undertaken a great many years ago by the Academy without any relevant monetary resources or indeed any approximate measurement of the time and labour involved. At long last a skilled part-time editor (Latham) had been discovered who, with financial support far below the minimum required (by 1961–2 it had dwindled to £150), was now struggling through the penultimate stages of a Revised Word-List. This might be expected, if and when achieved, to bring a little much-wanted encouragement into the main project—the Medieval Dictionary itself—if at the same time new blood could be poured into the veins of its governance. (A distinguished critic of it in September 1958 referred bluntly and truthfully to 'the extreme supineness of the Committee, which met the other day for the first time for two years'.) On the other hand, the Academy was simply not yet in a financial position to crack the whip with any real authority. All that could be attempted was to preserve the project from complete dissolution until three immediate objectives could be secured: (a) the completion of the long-deferred Revised Word-List, (b) an assurance that the part-time Editor, who behind the scenes had more than proved his worth, could assume full-time responsibility with the backing of a rejuvenated Committee, and, not least, (c) a guarantee of adequate funds.

During the following years all these objectives were in fact attained: in 1962 H.M. Treasury, as related in another chapter, for the first time allocated a substantial Research Grant to the Academy, and the Dictionary might expect to receive its share; in 1963 the Council of the Academy appointed a new Medieval Latin Dictionary Committee, its predecessor having revived sufficiently to commit hari-kari (the phrase *functus officio* was used); in 1965, as already told, the *Revised Word-List* was eventually and successfully published; and Mr. Latham foresaw the probability of being able to devote full time to the Dictionary after May 1967. The new Committee's first Chairman, F. J. E. Raby, who brought an extensive understanding of medieval Latin poetry to bear upon his new task, died in 1966 and was succeeded by Sir Roger Mynors. In his letter of modest acceptance (March 1967) Mynors wrote: 'The Dictionary will be a test case of the validity nowadays of the old English habit of doing things with a handful of amateurs on a shoestring and yet getting somewhere, and we *must* make a success of it'. Happily the shoestring is today appreciably more robust than the frail thread from which this story started. From the Academy's new Research Grant, the Dictionary received £1,200 annually from 1964 to 1966, in which year it was at long last elevated to the high status of a Major Research Project of the Academy. As such it was allocated £5,750 in 1967 and £6,110 in 1968. It is hoped that 1971 may welcome the first fascicules of its substantive publication, at any rate in proof form. Meanwhile the slips have been housed by the kindness of successive Deputy Keepers of the Public Records, with the liberal prospect thereafter of a free home in Lambeth Palace Library. It has been a long haul but the harbour is in sight.

(iii) THE OXYRHYNCHUS PAPYRI

The story of the discovery of writings on papyrus, with a general account of their treatment and interpretation, has been admirably told by Professor E. G. Turner, F.B.A.,[1] and need not here be repeated. Suffice it to recall that the incidental or accidental uncovering of these documents, mainly on Egyptian sites, encouraged in the 1890s a systematic search for them with an improving technology and an astonishing success. In particular the Egypt Exploration Fund, now the Egypt Exploration Society, in 1895 commissioned D. G. Hogarth, B. P. Grenfell, and A. S. Hunt of Oxford to conduct trial-excavations in an organized attempt to discover Greek and Roman papyri. The work was carried out largely by Grenfell and Hunt who in 1896–7 unearthed an immense quantity of papyri at the village of Behnesa, the ancient Oxyrhynchus, on the edge of the Western Desert 120 miles south of Cairo. After diversions to other sites, the two explorers returned to Oxyrhynchus in 1903 and continued to amass papyri there until 1907. In 1908 Grenfell fell ill and the concession was abandoned.

The first Grenfell–Hunt volume of the *Oxyrhynchus Papyri* appeared in 1898, and by 1966 no fewer than thirty-two volumes (some 3,000 papyri) had been published. The method adopted was: introduction, text, translation, and brief commentary, and papyrologists have regarded this as a model of its kind. But remarkable though the production has been both in pace and format, many boxfuls of fragments, mostly at Oxford, are still untreated, let alone published, and at the end of 1965 Professor Turner presented an appeal to the appropriate Section V (Classical Literature and Philology) of the Academy. He pointed out that the publication of the papyri had affected every branch of classical scholarship; indeed, some of the texts have caused a revolution in our knowledge. There is a large number both of complete documentary texts and of fragmentary manuscripts of works already known awaiting publication, and there are many texts of unknown authors. But the financial resources of the Egypt Exploration Society (the owners or trustees of the papyri) have always been limited to financing the actual cost of publication with nothing to spare for technical or secretarial assistance and only minute honoraria for the scholars responsible for the arduous work.

The supervision of the project was in the hands of an Oxyrhynchus Papyri Committee consisting of C. H. Roberts, T. C. Skeat, Professor J. W. B. Barns, and Professor P. H. J. Lloyd-Jones, with Professor Turner as Chairman. The preliminary problem was now being tackled in two ways: papyri relaxed but

[1] *Greek Papyri: an Introduction* (Oxford, 1968).

not yet published in Oxford were being roughly catalogued, and papyri not yet relaxed were being damped out partly in Oxford and partly in London. The experience of the past three years had shown that preparations for publication would now proceed more quickly and involve a wider circle of scholars than hitherto. As the inventory progressed, information from it could be made more readily available. But the whole procedure demanded a committee responsible to the Academy working through a paid secretary. Incidentally, all unpublished texts ought to be photographed. The over-all cost of the enterprise would be something like £5,000 a year.

The proposal was welcomed by Section V in January 1966 and was provisionally included by Council in February (subject to favourable reception by the Research Committee) amongst the Academy's Major Research Projects. At its March meeting the Research Committee approved; and in May the Council allotted the Oxyrhynchus Papyri Committee a grant of £3,800. To the Committee already serving and now formally absorbed by the Academy the name of Mr. W. S. Barrett was added. Future volumes would be published by the Egypt Exploration Society 'for the British Academy'.

The procedures and personnel of the project as now reconstituted along the lines proposed by Professor Turner were agreed at a meeting of the Committee held in the Clarendon Press, Oxford, on 8 June 1966. Thereafter, work has continued smoothly and three new volumes (XXXIII–XXXV) have been published between October 1968 and January 1969. They well illustrate the continuing importance of the series. Volume XXXIII (P. Parsons, Dr. John Rea, and Professor Turner) includes two texts of Menander's *Misoumenos*, a text of his *Carthaginian*, and new fragments of his *Kolax*. Volume XXXIV (L. Ingrams, Dr. P. Kingston, P. Parsons, and Dr. John Rea) has miscellaneous texts, including a large new fragment of Oxyrhynchus papyrus I.9, which now presents a continuous setting-out of a knowledgeable ancient writer's opinion on certain difficult metrical questions. Volume XXXV, by Mr. Edgar Lobel who has long done invaluable work on the Greek literary papyri, contains some new early choral lyric poetry and interesting commentaries on Old Comedy. And further volumes are on the way.

On the financial side details will not be expected here, but it is worth noting that the adequate staffing of the enterprise has at last been ensured by the Academy, which allotted to it £3,560 in 1967 and a similar sum in the following year. At the same time the

University of Cambridge has contributed substantially to editorial expenses, the University of Oxford provides a room in the Ashmolean Museum and pays the salary of a technical assistant, whilst University College, London, also supplies a room and the services of a research assistant. Furthermore, the Egypt Exploration Society currently continues to bear the full costs of printing. On the whole, for the moment at least *Oxyrhynchus* may be modestly described as a well-furnished project.

(iv) ENGLISH PLACE-NAMES

For a period which approaches half a century the frequent volumes of the English Place-Name Society have been a feature of the British historical and topographical scene. Their appeal has indeed reached far beyond the hidden dens of scholarship. Any intelligent dweller of the English landscape cannot fail to find a new enrichment of his environment in the down-to-earth descriptive or personal names which from age to age have taken root around him. Under scrupulous analysis by the devoted band of students who have since 1923 collected and presented them, these names have become a veritable dictionary of the countryside and a pattern of cyclic settlement within it. That the great project should in these latter years look increasingly towards the Academy for patronage and provision is wholly apposite. Much has been done but much still remains to do.

The introductory volume (1924 and reprints), edited by (Sir) Allen Mawer and (Sir) Frank Stenton, bore a pious dedication 'To the Memory of Henry Bradley, Greatest of English Place-Name Scholars'. Bradley had died the year before and so failed to participate in the inauguration of an enterprise which would have been very close to his heart and, in a sensible measure, the fruition of his life-long interest. In and after 1924 many hands and minds contributed to the work: notably Mawer and Stenton, Eilert Ekwall, James Tait, and A. H. Smith, who, for an active sixteen years, was the Society's Director and general manager. The long series of county surveys began in 1925 with *The Place-Names of Buckinghamshire* under the joint editorship of Mawer and Stenton; and now (1968–9) the substantive volumes are being supplemented by *The Journal of the English Place-Name Society* as a vehicle for additions and corrections.

The Academy's Place-Name file is, as might be expected, largely a litter of financial minutiae, with the assumption that, save for an occasional reminder, the academic achievement spoke for itself. The first surviving entry, dated 10 June 1944, is an acknowledgement to Kenyon from Stenton of 'the good news that the Council has renewed its grant of £150' to the Society. Thereafter until 1957 the Academy continued to renew this exiguous annual allocation from its very inadequate sources. Even so, there was a passing phase of uneasiness in regard to the Society's administrative effectiveness, and the Academy's Secretary sent his friend Sir Cyril Fox the Society's Report for private comment. Fox's reply (January 1951) was:

I feel I have been smacked in the face by a dead fish . . . The Victorian set-up of the damned report! Hasn't altered since the Society was founded. Nobody *cares* whether it produces new subscribers or not. *But* the Society does vitally important work as we both know. Historians and archaeologists need the county volumes directly they are done and lament when they aren't. . . .

And so forth. Meanwhile the Secretary had demanded from the Society's Treasurer a categorical statement of financial policy:

I see that you will have to raise about £1,750. At the most only a relatively small portion of this sum can be expected at present from the Academy. . . . It would probably help our Council if you could indicate the kind of resources from which you expect to obtain the remainder. The programme seems to be a little vague! In short, the general impression received is that the whole thing needs tightening up and invigorating. . . .

The upshot was that the Society appointed a new Director in A. H. Smith, Quain Professor of English Language and Literature at University College, and, with what were hoped to be encouraging exhortations from the Academy, things rapidly improved. Adequate funds were scraped together for continuing publication; in 1958 the Academy's symbolical grant was enlarged to the princely total of £200, and the energetic new Director found the rest. By 1966 the Society could at last report that it had caught up its arrears of publications and that, for the next few years at any rate, regular production seemed assured. This happy announcement preceded by all too short a space the very melancholy one of the sudden death (in May 1967) of the Director who had striven so arduously and successfully to bring new life to the project.

In one way and another the year 1967–8 turned out to be critical in the history of the Society. The death of A. H. Smith was followed in June by that of Sir Frank Stenton, the Society's veteran President. In October its admirable Treasurer found it necessary to retire, and in January 1968, died one of the project's principal contributors, Dr. P. H. Reaney. These various casualties, all within the space of nine months, involved more than the loss of the Society's most senior and experienced scholars. In particular, Smith as Director had been able to afford to the Society's research and office-work some part of the services of the research and secretarial assistants appointed from time to time by University College to the Quain Professor. Now, though the business office of the Society remained at University College, the assistance formerly concentrated there was dispersed or discontinued. In an inevitable welter of reorganization, the culminating loss of A. H. Smith was manifest at every point.

But the new team, with Professor Dorothy Whitelock as Stenton's Presidential successor, lost little time in tackling the situation. In December 1967 Professor Whitelock addressed a strongly reasoned appeal to the Academy, asking for an appreciably increased grant-in-aid sufficient to provide the secretarial and research assistances essential for the considerable task of collecting and preparing the materials for the twenty counties which still remained outstanding. Her concluding trumpet-call surely deserves an echo:

It is feared by the Council of the Society that, unless some such augmentation of the Society's resources is obtained soon, the good record and efficient conduct of the Survey of English Place-Names may break down. This would be a sad end to forty years' hard work, a disaster to those concerned with the Survey and the Society, a loss to the world of learning, and a breach of faith with those eminent toponymists and Academicians who established this branch of scholarship so many years ago.

The call was heard: in May 1968 the Academy's Council raised the Society's grant to £1,500, and there is (1969) a whisper of the possible conferment on the Place-Names of the title or sobriquet of Major Research Project of the Academy. The list which Professor Whitelock appended to her petition, of forty-three published volumes and of eight others in preparation surely deserves that (it is to be hoped) rewarding accolade.

(v) MEDIEVAL STAINED GLASS

If the wholesale destruction of medieval stained glass during the Second World War were not sufficient incentive in itself, any serious project for the comprehensive recording of surviving material of this fragile and gracious kind would commend itself as an overdue and essential contribution to art-history and iconography. It was in fact left to the Comité International d'Histoire de l'Art (C.I.H.A.) at Berne in 1951 to make the first practical proposal for a corpus of medieval stained glass on an international scale. And in 1954 the Union Académique Internationale (U.A.I.), after securing the unanimous consent of its member-academies, lent prestige to the proposal by adding it to the fifteen other enterprises then under its patronage. By so doing it was able to obtain from UNESCO through the Conseil International de la Philosophie et des Sciences Humaines (C.I.P.S.H.) an initial grant of $1,000 for each of two annual volumes during the period 1954–7.

In its early days the project was actively supported by France, Germany, Austria, Switzerland, and Italy. Others followed, and in November 1955 steps were taken to involve Great Britain. Professor Dr. Hans R. Hahnloser, Treasurer-Secretary of C.I.H.A., wrote to Sir Charles Webster and Professor (Sir) Roger Mynors—both of them closely interested in the U.A.I. and its children—a reasoned plea to interest the British Academy in the matter and a request for advice in the formation of a National Committee to organize the British contribution.

It is fair to say that the British reaction to the invitation was concisely expressed by Roger Mynors: 'Glorious Idea. But what do we use for money?' That wise observation (incidentally from one to whom, in spite of his protest that it was no business of his except as an amateur, the project in its early stages owed much helpful counsel) marked the beginning of a somewhat lengthy but ultimately successful series of interchanges which may in the long view be profitably curtailed. Briefly, the matter was referred in proper routine to Section XI (History of Art) which, on 11 January 1956, gave 'full support to the project for the Corpus Vitrearum' and proposed the setting-up of a national committee for Great Britain. A week later the Council of the Academy agreed, and proposed as members of the committee: Professor Francis Wormald (Chairman), Professor (Sir) Anthony Blunt, E. A. Lane (Victoria and Albert Museum), Professor (Sir) Roger Mynors, Dr. W. Oakeshott (Rector of Lincoln College), G. F. Webb, Dr. Christopher Woodforde, and Dr. G. Zarnecki. Dr. Oakeshott declined membership, not from lack of interest but because of an excess of it; as a Pilgrim Trustee he anticipated a somewhat embarrassing personal position if the new

Committee should, as it might well do, see fit to approach his Trust for funds.

The British participation was now nominally on its feet; it still had to learn to walk. From its first meeting on 5 July 1956, the Corpus Vitrearum Committee under the vigorous leadership of Professor Wormald got down to work upon its two initial problems: organization and finance. A year later (2 July 1957) it was able to record appreciable action under both heads.

As to organization, with his welcome consent the Revd. Dr. Christopher Woodforde of New College, as the foremost English scholar in the field, had been saddled with the task of the preliminary survey of England, county by county, to discover approximately how much medieval glass had already been discovered and photographed. His report was not encouraging. A great part of the problem still remained quite untouched and such of the work as had been attempted in the past was largely superficial. It was recommended that, as a first requisite, a 'pilot' volume should be prepared covering the glass of three counties: Berkshire, Buckinghamshire, and Oxfordshire which, it was thought, would provide both a fair sample of the fragmentary material, still largely unknown, in village churches, and also (in Oxford itself) some well preserved and well documented glass of high quality. Apart from Oxford, this would mean the examination and recording roughly of 65 'vitriferous' churches in Berkshire, 65 in Buckinghamshire, and 80 in Oxfordshire. Such a 'pilot' volume would provide not only a part of the Corpus but would enable the Committee to formulate a considered policy for the rest of the scheme.

An investigating staff of three persons would be required: a director of the survey (Dr. Woodforde), a photographer, and a draughtsman. Towards this staff and its equipment, the Director of the Courtauld Institute (Sir Anthony Blunt) offered the Committee the use of the Institute's photographer, together with the Institute's photographic van. But there would remain the appreciable costs of travelling and other incidental expenses, and the total annual sum foreseen was unlikely to be less than £1,650.

This raised the thorny question of finance. Here the Council of the Academy, whether prompted or by its own normal prevision, had already on the 22 May 1957 'agreed to authorise the officers at their discretion to forward to the Pilgrim Trust an application, to be submitted by the Corpus Vitrearum Committee, for a grant towards the preparation of a pilot volume on the medieval glass of Berks, Bucks and Oxon'. At its meeting on 2 July, the Committee approved a manifesto for submission to the long-suffering Pilgrims, and this, suitably wrapped up, was sent by the Academy's Secretary to Lord Kilmaine as Secretary of the Pilgrim Trust on 8 July. The reply was immediate and showed the Trust's traditional and instant understanding: 'I am glad to be able to tell you that my Trustees voted a grant of £1,650 towards the preparation of material for a "pilot" volume ... I enclose a cheque for £1,650.' The date was the 1 August 1957.

All should now have been well, for a while, in respect of the pilot scheme. But alas it was not. Disastrously, the chief pilot himself fell overboard. In 1959 Christopher Woodforde was translated to the Deanery of Wells and medieval glass knew him no more. In fact, for some time before his departure very little of a practical kind had happened to his special project. Time slipped by, not (as will shortly be seen) in utter idleness but without determined direction. At last, on the 12 July 1961, the Committee clearly and firmly reviewed the whole situation and in effect prepared for a fresh start.

First there was the languishing pilot scheme. The remedy was not, in principle, hard to see. In his report to the Academy's Secretary on 17 July 1961, Professor Wormald observed:

The Committee was quite clear that the scheme for producing any volume of the Corpus will be wrecked if there cannot be someone who can work on the job full-time. The whole study of glass in this country has been for years hag-ridden by amateurs, and I for one am convinced that we shall never get anywhere unless we can have somebody doing it all the time. Peter Newton, a young student of the Courtauld Institute who has just completed a large thesis on stained glass in the Midlands, would do this very well. . . . What we should like is for the Academy to employ him full-time for X number of years.

Meanwhile, Peter Newton secured a Research Fellowship at the Barber Institute at Birmingham for the next two years and during that period would be in a position, for the refund of expenses only, to complete or at least to continue intermittently the delayed pilot scheme.

And so from the end of August 1961 preliminary work on the three counties was resumed under the new leadership. On the 6 November, Wormald wrote: 'Newton has found that there are a great many more churches in those counties having fragments of ancient glass than either Woodforde or Mynors suspected. . . . So you can see that we are not really in a position to do much at the minute about asking for money . . .' It became rapidly clear, however, that more money was precisely the urgent

pre-condition now required for sustained progress. Above all, it
was essential to provide for and to regularize the services of P. A.
Newton for a period of at least three years; i.e. well beyond the
term of his fellowship. Accordingly, in February 1962 Professor
Wormald concluded a further review with a demand for 'a grant
from the Academy of £1,300 per annum for three years in order
to complete the pilot volume'. The reply from the Academy's
Secretary was:

> May I say, with every possible and rather special goodwill to the
> *Vitreae,* that there is not the slightest hope of getting £1,300 out of
> the Academy for this scheme. Whitehall is very rigorous this year in the
> matter of grants. . . . But this does mean looking elsewhere. Incidentally
> I understand that there is a balance in hand of £1,230 from the Pilgrim
> Trust grant. If this amount could now be extended to cover three years
> at the same figure per annum, we should have time to look round for
> other sources . . .

Briefly again, Wormald and the Secretary once more approached our faithfullest friends the Pilgrims, with the happy
sequel that a letter from Lord Kilmaine to the Secretary on
15 May 1962 contained the following generous sentence: 'My
Trustees were glad to vote a further grant of £2,000 to provide
the salary of Dr. P. A. Newton at the rate of £1,000 p.a. for the
two years 1963–64 and 1964–65, it being understood that you
already have a more than sufficient balance from our previous
grant to cover the salary for 1962–63'. It may here be added that
in August 1962 C.I.P.S.H. added a contribution of $925 to the
Committee's voracious purse.

As things turned out, Dr. Newton did not begin full-time work
for the Corpus Vitrearum Committee until the 1 January 1964,
when for administrative convenience he was attached to the
Courtauld Institute. By the end of that year he was able to report
that the medieval glass in the city and county of Oxford had all
been noted and photographed. Financial provision was still
available from the Pilgrim donation for 1965, and work proceeded
on iconographical and other aspects of the Oxford material. And
then in November the Committee was confronted by a second
set-back: the invaluable Dr. Newton was appointed to a Lectureship in the University of York. Happily this event did not
completely sever his association with the pilot project, which continues to profit from time to time from his interest and intervention. But it did necessarily interfere with the smooth development
of the work, and was a factor in its displacement as a priority
scheme by another great enterprise which had since 1961 given

considerable exercise to the minds of the Committee. Additional delay in 1968 was occasioned by Dr. Newton's illness, though in January 1969 the Committee was able to see and approve a specimen 'opening' of the Oxford volume.

Reference has been made above to an important meeting of the Committee on the 12 July 1961 when there was a general stock-taking of the progress (or otherwise) of the Glass project as a whole. An item on the agenda was 'Correspondence with the Provost of King's College, Cambridge', and eight or nine years later the substance of that correspondence still shapes the Committee's proceedings.

The gist of the Provost's (Noel Annan's) letters was first that Mr. Hilary Wayment, an authority on the stained glass of King's College chapel, had asked him whether the College would be prepared to help him financially in the preparation and publishing of a major work on the glass, and secondly, was there any chance of the photographs of the glass, with Wayment's text, being published in the *Corpus Vitrearum Medii Aevi*. If there were, it would be a mistake to envisage independent publication.

Professor Wormald's replies were (*a*) that certainly Wayment's project was worthy of encouragement, but (*b*) that the *Corpus* was being produced under the auspices of UNESCO who would be expected to give a grant towards publication but would not assist in any preparatory work such as salaries, expenses, and photography. These charges fell upon each country participating in the scheme. Moreover, whilst some money for publication could be got from UNESCO, the balance would have to be found from English sources. But he would like to refer the correspondence to the British Academy.

To the Academy's Secretary, Wormald wrote (21 June 1961):

It seems to me that we are being offered *gratis*, as far as preparation and photography are concerned, a volume which would certainly be (*a*) very splendid to look at, (*b*) very useful. With everyone working on 16th century mannerist art we should get here a volume which would certainly excite a good deal of interest and would incidentally be dealing with a single 16th century monument of prime importance. It does appear, however, that while King's will be ready and willing to support the preparation of the volume as well as making the remarkable set of photographs which they have available, they may well jib at paying for the whole publication. . . . I imagine that UNESCO would do something for us, but I am pretty certain that the UNESCO contribution would not cover the whole of publication expenditure. I cannot imagine that at this stage the Academy could agree to publishing the volume. On the other hand I should like to be able to encourage the Provost. . . .

To this the Secretary:

The correspondence seems to me to carry the matter far enough to enable the Committee to make a fairly solid resolution for our Council at its next meeting. Meanwhile we must keep Annan gently on the boil.

In reporting the meeting of the Corpus Vitrearum Committee on 12 July 1961, Professor Wormald records that the King's College Cambridge glass

was discussed very fully and by good fortune Kenneth Harrison, formerly of King's, who knows a good deal about the glass, was present. He has been discussing the whole question with the Provost and put forward an alternative suggestion to the one originally given to us, namely that the King's windows should be a joint effort in which Arthur Lane[1] should make a description of the windows and Wayment, who, as you may remember, was to have done the whole of the description and the art-historical introduction, should confine himself to the art-historical introduction alone. This would be a good arrangement, because Lane is very well acquainted with the King's glass and has already done some descriptions of it. On the other hand Wayment knows the whole history of North French and Belgian glass-painting extremely well and has also an excellent knowledge of late Flemish art, which is essential for anybody studying the King's windows. The financial arrangements, of course, remain to be worked out, but it is possible that King's would be prepared to assist with Lane's expenses and I have even suggested in a letter to the Provost that he would require some sort of honorarium. Wayment would certainly need paying as well. From what Harrison says it seems clear that King's, if it was to pay for the expenses of producing the material, would be reluctant to pay for the actual printing and production of the book, and presumably the Academy would have to raise some funds for this. After all the scheme for the Corpus Vitrearum has been officially adopted by the Academy and we may assume that it will expect to pay some parts of the cost. I have written to the Provost on these lines. I hope I have not gone too far!

Once more to summarize: work on the King's glass eventually got under way approximately along the lines suggested. In January 1969 Mr. Wayment was able to report the completion of the physical survey of the glass, a task in which he had had the advantage of the co-operation of Mr. Dennis King who, as an experimental restorer of ancient glass, had been an exceedingly useful

[1] Died in 1963. Thereafter in fact Hilary Wayment catalogued the glass and Kenneth Harrison prepared the art-historical introduction.

associate (later member) of the Committee since 1965. Amongst the new findings in the process of this work, it was of interest to note:

i. The identification of one of the glaziers with an anonymous Fleming whose work is also to be seen in the church at Fairford, Gloucestershire.

ii. The probability that much of the work of restoration previously assumed to belong to the nineteenth century derives in fact from the eighteenth century or earlier, and that the eighteenth century glaziers, though ill supplied in pot-metal, showed an unsuspected skill in painting and staining white glass for replacements.

iii. The proof of Mr. C. Morris's theory that the figure of Solomon (above the Adoration of the Magi) was also intended to represent King Henry VIII.[1]

iv. New evidence, gleaned from the archives in Amsterdam and Antwerp, on the life of Dieric Vellart, the presumed designer of most of the great windows.

At this point, the Corpus Vitrearum passes out of the present chronicle, leaving the Committee, under its devoted Chairman, busily beginning to feed the King's volume into the Oxford University Press and simultaneously, no doubt, occupied no less busily with the eternal and merciless but never insoluble problems of finance.

The present recorder would add a final *cri de coeur*, final in the present context but actually dating back to 6 August 1957. On that day I wrote a word of thanks to Francis Wormald in acknowledgement of his characteristic congratulations on our securing the interest of the Pilgrim Trust:

Thank you for your kindly note. I, too, am delighted that the Pilgrim Trust saw the light even through stained glass darkly. But one thing does rather concern me in the matter of this survey. Under modern conditions no photographic survey *unless in colour* will conform with the sort of standards we should set ourselves. I am firmly convinced that every piece of stained glass worthy of individual record should be photographed in colour, now. Even though this will add appreciably to the cost of the whole business, the answer is, Get more money for it and do it properly while we are about it.

In 1969 this is even truer and more feasible than in 1957. But the published volumes make in this regard a poor showing. For example at random, the fat Vol. III of Switzerland has only 18

---

[1] An identification which I am reluctantly unable to find convincing.

plates in colour as against 236 plates in black and white; France I has 8 in colour and 101 in black and white; Austria I has 8 in colour and 24 plates + 309 figs. in black and white. All this and more is below the modern standard; well below the standard required of so essentially colourful a material. It still remains to be seen how far the first English volume will supersede this dreary and archaic norm.

(vi) BRITISH COINS

Since 1931 Greek coins housed in public and less permanent private collections have been systematically illustrated—on beautiful folio pages where a neat rivulet of text meanders beside a meadow of money—under the sobriquet of *Sylloge Nummorum Graecorum*. Mostly this Sylloge has been published in the name of the British Academy, though occasional volumes or fascicules have been issued elsewhere, in Berlin, Klagenfurt, New York. The inspired genius behind the scheme has from the outset been Dr. E. S. G. Robinson, sometime Keeper of the Coins and Medals at the British Museum. Not satisfied by this extended labour, in May 1952 Dr. Robinson wrote to the Secretary of the Academy as follows:

A group of English numismatists have raised the question of a series of publications of English coins on the lines, *mutatis mutandis*, of *Sylloge Nummorum Graecorum*. It is a project very desirable to embark upon. The Greek Sylloge is more and more proving its value as a collection of materials, and the conditions which brought it forth are operating with equal force in the study of English numismatics. Big private collections are being broken up, and I do not suppose will be formed again on the same scale. They are mostly sold at auction, with inadequate catalogues from the scientific point of view. The important coins scientifically are, as often as not, not collectors' pieces and are apt to get overlooked. Also, as in Greek numismatics, the study of dies in this series is becoming of the first importance, and, in order to pursue it a large mass of material photographically illustrated is necessary. Great strides are now being made, particularly in the study of Anglo-Saxon coins, and the results for history in general and even for the history of art will be important. The experience gained with the Sylloge will certainly suggest modifications of the original lay-out and means of cutting the expenses of publication, which are now mounting so high. I have been asked to explore the probability of the Academy undertaking to sponsor a series of this kind parallel with the Greek Sylloge. . . .

The Secretary's unhesitating reply was:

It seems to me to be an excellent idea, and I will bring it up to the Council. It will probably be referred to Section X (Archaeology), and meanwhile it would be extremely useful if you could find time to draft a summary scheme relating (*a*) to the Editorship (if possible, would you suggest the scope of the first two volumes?), and (*b*) the sort of cost involved? This seems to me exactly the kind of thing that the Academy should do.

So also thought the Academy's Council which, after receiving the approval of Sections X and XI (History of Art), gave its general blessing in May 1953 to the proposed *Sylloge Nummorum Britannicorum*, shortly and sensibly to be re-christened the *Sylloge of Coins of the British Isles*. In the absence of funds and a more detailed programme the Council abstained from adding administrative to moral patronage pending such time as the scheme might have sorted itself out amongst the specialist institutions and individuals concerned. But for the nonce the Olympian nod was enough. The promoters proceeded, with application if without unnecessary haste, to assemble an informal Committee under the Chairmanship of Sir Frank Stenton and including Christopher Blunt, R. H. M. Dolley, Philip Grierson, of course E. S. G. Robinson, Dorothy Whitelock and others, and P. D. Whitting, G.M., undertook the Honorary Secretaryship. Discussions were held and in the autumn of 1955 more regular meetings of what may be called the Shadow-Committee met to consider definite priorities of preparation and publication, having regard to the perennial bogey of finance. The minutiae of this procedure, in so far as they were recorded, need not be repeated here; but, in response to an inquiry as to progress from the Academy's Secretary in October 1955, Stenton reported that the project was now rapidly taking shape: a list of collections which it was desirable to review had been prepared, and even a specimen page had been considered. 'It is clear to all of us that the Sylloge, though a long-term project, is practicable, and that it will produce results of value to students working in many different fields.' And he added: 'On the other hand we feel that the Committee directing it needs some assurance of permanence such as it does not at present possess. . . . I am therefore writing to ask if you would bring before the Council our unanimous request that a formal liaison should be established between the Academy and the Committee.' (It may be interpolated that there had previously been some discussion as to whether the project should seek adoption by the Academy or by the Society of Antiquaries.) At its meeting on 18 January 1956 the Council of the Academy was pleased to admit the Sylloge Committee as a Committee of the Academy.

So far so good. True, there still remained the ultimate question of funds—a traditional Academy problem which was not to approach any substantial solution for another half-dozen years. Nevertheless, progress soon began to show, and all credit is due to the Committee, not least to its Secretary, for the fact that between 1956 and 1969 no fewer than twelve splendidly illustrated and annotated volumes have appeared in its name. Particularly in the early years this was not an easy task. The begging-bowl was passed round with shameless persistence. For the first volume, illustrating the Ancient British and Anglo-Saxon coins of the Fitzwilliam Museum at Cambridge by Philip Grierson, the Museum itself could offer no more than the casts of the coins; but the British Numismatic Society weighed in with a contribution, the Academy allocated grants of £200 in 1957 and £250 in 1958, and other gifts accrued. Naturally until publication (in November 1958) the balm of sales-income could not begin to alleviate the situation but somehow or other the Committee and its harassed Secretary Whitting contrived to survive. By 1959 the worst moment was past.

Meanwhile the Committee was looking and working ahead. The preparation of the first volume of the Anglo-Saxon coins in the Hunterian and Coats collections at Glasgow was proceeding rapidly under Anne Robertson; and Stenton had already approached the Trustees of the British Museum for approval and help for the inclusion of their appropriate collections in the series. Both projects came duly to fruition and were acclaimed: The Glasgow collections in 1961 and the British Museum Hiberno-Norse coins, by R. H. M. Dolley, then of the Department of Coins and Medals, in 1966—incidentally at the cost of the Trustees, who thereby became the publishers, but in the series. And there were other irons in the fire. At the suggestion of Mr. Dolley, Stenton in September 1959 made contact with the Danish National Museum at Copenhagen with a view to incorporating in the Sylloge the Ancient British and Anglo-Saxon coins in the Royal Danish Collection. The proposal was welcomed, and Dr. Georg Galster, formerly Keeper of the Collection, lent his scholarship and experience to the work. In anticipation it may be recorded that when in 1965–6 indebtedness again raised its head, in connection with Copenhagen II, the Carlsberg Foundation and other Danish benefactors came to the rescue with welcome contributions. By this time, too, the Academy's allocation had reached the £1,000 level. Vagaries in the rate of publication are naturally reflected in the financial vicissitudes of the project, but there is a special pleasure in recording the energy and responsibility which have marked it administratively from the beginning and, above all, the success of its output.

For there is no doubt that the Sylloge has attained and holds in its way a unique place in modern numismatic scholarship as the provider of systematically organized and presented material for further research or reference. From the outset its format has been royal-octavo, as suitable to its contents and as less unwieldy than the folio of its eminent Greek prototype. Moreover, it tends in comparison to have a little more meat on its bones. Brief historical accounts of the individual collections may be provided; notes added on particular features of certain of the series; lists of sources appended; and finally there is a reasonably full apparatus page by page. All this inclines to more generosity, at least to a little less austerity, than those great albums from which it is in a sense derived. Occasional volumes indeed swell to the dimension of a pioneer treatise, as, notably, D. F. Allen's intriguing isolation and discussion of the tribal coins of the midland Coritani. Of the Sylloge's over-all scope so far a summary list of its publications to 1969 is its most eloquent testimony and may here with all proper admiration be displayed:

1. Fitzwilliam Museum, Cambridge.
   Part I. *Ancient British and Anglo-Saxon Coins.*
   By Philip Grierson, 1958.

2. The Hunterian Museum, Glasgow.
   Part I. *The Anglo-Saxon Coins in the Hunterian and Coats Collections.*
   By Anne S. Robertson, 1961.

3. *The Coins of the Coritani.*
   By D. F. Allen, 1963.

4. The Royal Danish Coin Collection, Copenhagen.
   Part I. *Ancient British and Anglo-Saxon Coins.*
   By Georg Galster, 1964.

5. Grosvenor Museum, Chester.
   Part I. *The Willoughby Gardner Collection of Coins with the Chester Mint Signature.*
   By Elizabeth J. E. Pirie, 1964.

6. National Museum of Antiquities of Scotland, Edinburgh.
   Part I. *Anglo-Saxon Coins (with associated Foreign Coins).*
   By R. B. K. Stevenson, 1966.

7. The Royal Danish Collection, Copenhagen.
Part II. *Anglo-Saxon Coins. Aethelred II.*
By Georg Galster, 1966.

8. The Hiberno-Norse Coins in the British Museum.
By R. H. M. Dolley, 1966.

9. Ashmolean Museum, Oxford.
Part I. *Anglo-Saxon Pennies.*
By J. D. A. Thompson, 1967.

10. Ulster Museum, Belfast.
Anglo-Saxon Coins, John–Edward III.
By M. Dolley and W. Seaby, 1968.

11. Reading University.
Anglo-Saxon and Norman Coins.
Royal Coin Cabinet, Stockholm.
Anglo-Norman Pennies.
By C. E. Blunt and M. Dolley, 1969.

12. Ashmolean Museum, Oxford.
Part II. *English Coins, 1066–1279.*
By D. M. Metcalf, 1969.

(vii) THE WORKS AND CORRESPONDENCE OF JEREMY BENTHAM

In the earlier and basically more important paragraphs of this section, my pen has been most generously assumed by Lord Robbins, who, with Professor J. H. Burns, has placed his knowledge at my disposal with the readiness and punctuality for which I have been constantly indebted through the years. His contribution is acknowledged more specifically by enclosure within inverted commas.

'If you are a visitor to the west end of the Cloisters at University College London, you may notice an erection resembling a large telephone kiosk without windows. If the doors thereof were to be opened, it would be revealed that this was the repository of the mortal remains of Jeremy Bentham who, although not a founder of the College, was the inspiration of those of his disciples who were, and whose body, after suitable operations, was presented to the College by one of them, Dr. Southwood Smith. There he sits, in appropriate early nineteenth century attire, a broad brimmed hat on his waxen face. Within living memory, it was the custom at annual meetings of the Fellows of the College to wheel him into a position at the festive board. But since the Second World War this custom has fallen into desuetude and on such occasions he is now present only in the Senior Common Room, whither the Fellows repair after the main banquet.

'Much more important than this rather odd inheritance, however, is the existence in the College library of a vast mass of Bentham manuscripts covering a working life of sixty years, devoted almost exclusively to the elaboration of drafts on an immense range of subjects relating to almost every conceivable aspect of society: criminal, civil and constitutional law, judicial procedure, economic and social problems, education, language, logic, ethics, and religion. There are other collections of Bentham manuscripts, both at the British Museum and at Geneva. But the main repository is at University College; and it is safe to say that no more important accumulation of material relating to the history of social ideas in the latter part of the eighteenth and the early part of the nineteenth century is in existence anywhere in the world.

'At Bentham's death in 1832, his literary executor was John Bowring, relations between Bentham and some of his abler disciples, conspicuously the Mills, having become perceptibly cooler in the last few years of his life. Bowring was to achieve some distinction in public life, as an M.P., as British consul at Canton, and as Governor of Hong Kong (receiving a knighthood on the occasion of this appointment in 1854). He was also very active in the beginnings of the campaign for the decimalization of the British coinage. But as a literary executor he had severe shortcomings. It is clear from his edition of Bentham's *Deontology* (published in 1834, but not reproduced in the collected edition which followed a few years later) that he had no strong feelings of obligation to be faithful to the original text. It is clear too that he felt at liberty to publish or not publish according to his conceptions of the appropriate, and that his own command of literary technique was, to put it mildly, primitive. That the edition of Jeremy Bentham's works which was published in eleven volumes between 1838 and 1843 was not even more disastrous, both from the scholarly and from the literary point of view, than it in fact was, is due less to Bowring than to his collaborators. These—notably John Hill Burton, the leading Scottish Benthamite and later historiographer royal of Scotland—did most of the effective editing, under what the title-pages call Bowring's "superintendence". The result, in double columns of small print, left much to be desired. Manuscript material was extensively edited and rearranged without any indication of what had been omitted and what inserted. Important groups of manuscript were totally ignored, and—a fact for which Bowring was evidently responsible —substantial published works of Bentham, especially on religion and the church, were omitted altogether from the collection. Finally, the edition closed with Bowring's "Memoirs of Bentham" —a biography which has a fair claim to be regarded as the worst biography of an important personage in the English language.

'It was from Bowring, on his departure from China in 1849, that the main body of Bentham's manuscripts passed into the custody of University College. It is something of a scandal that for the next hundred years or more no systematic use was made of the original manuscripts. From time to time they were consulted by international scholars. On two occasions Professor Everett of Columbia University was successful in unearthing extremely important unpublished material—criticisms of Blackstone's *Commentaries* of which the famous *Fragment on Government* was only a part, and a sequel to *The Principles of Morals and Legislation* which, of course, was the main exposition from his own pen of Bentham's central position as regards ethics and jurisprudence; and there were other explorations of sectional fields. In 1937 Mr. Taylor Milne made a general catalogue of the material; but the greater part of it remained unstudied and unedited. The excuse made for this reproach to scholarship was that the range was so vast that no single editor could conceivably have tackled the whole of it. But the fact remains that the work of the man who is entitled to be regarded perhaps as the greatest jurist writing in the English language, and certainly one of the most notable influences in the history of social and political thought anywhere, remained without adequate presentation.

'In 1959, however, as a result of the initiative of Professor A. J. Ayer, the authorities of University College, led enthusiastically by the then Provost, now Lord Evans of Hungershall, set up a national committee to remedy this state of affairs by setting in motion the labours necessary to produce a complete collected edition of all available Bentham material. The committee was headed by Lord Cohen, who was succeeded in 1967 by Lord Robbins, and included leading international experts in the relevant fields from London, Oxford, Cambridge, and Columbia. Dr., now Professor, J. H. Burns of University College was appointed as General Editor. University College provided the necessary accommodation to house the secretariat, and through the years has made substantial subsidies to its upkeep. At the beginning, a generous contribution was made by the Rockefeller Foundation and, more recently, the Pilgrim Trust has assisted the enterprise with a direct subvention of £1,000 a year for five years from 1966. The Senate of the University of London has rendered solid support by providing to its Athlone Press advances of working capital to make a publication possible. There were also important contributions from an anonymous donor.

'To appreciate the magnitude of the labours involved, it must be realized that Bentham's handwriting is as difficult to decipher as a medieval palimpsest and that there are no less than 75,000 sheets of it in the College alone, as distinct from those available at other centres. The copying thereof in itself is a labour of years. On top of this are immense scholarly difficulties of disentangling from the works published by Bowring and elsewhere Bentham's final thoughts on the subjects concerned from the re-arrangements, alterations, and additions inserted, not only by Bowring but by those of his followers, such as Dumont, George Grote, J. S. Mill, and Francis Place, who were employed during Bentham's lifetime to piece together his drafts. It is estimated that at least thirty-eight volumes will be necessary to complete the presentation and it is unlikely that the work can be finished in much less than twenty-five years.

'From the beginning the Academy was involved in this important undertaking. Professor Ayer, Professor Hampshire, Professor Hart, and Lord Robbins, all Fellows of the Academy, have been members of the national committee since its inception. The Academy made a contribution of £250 from its then very exiguous fund towards the initial cost of examination and collation, and through the intervening years it has voted subsidies rising from £750 in 1964-5 to £1,500 (once £2,000) in 1966-7. Quite recently it has conferred on these activities the status of a Major Research Project: signifying that it will be regarded as having some prior claim to consideration when the grants for research are reviewed by the Council year by year.'

In 1968 the firstfruits were upon the table: two volumes of *The Correspondence of Jeremy Bentham*, edited by Dr. Timothy L. S. Sprigge. The letters, most of them previously unpublished, range from 1752, when Jeremy was in his fourth year, to 1780, and are a fascinating and astonishing miscellany of endearing youthfulness and the most mature precocity. They begin substantially with his residence at The Queen's College, Oxford, where he arrived at the age of twelve in time to add his contribution of Alcaic verses to the pious fascicule which the occasion of the death of the monarch in that year demanded, beginning (as he told his friend Bowring) 'Eheu Georgi' and 'certifying and proclaiming the experienced attributes of the dead god and the surely expected ditto of the living one'!

It is difficult even in this summary record to refrain from quoting from these Oxford letters. Day after day he spends hours translating and commenting upon Cicero's *Tusculan Questions* for the benefit of his admiring but demanding father. In the midst of preparing an eloquent Latin declamation on the evils of bodily indulgence and especially of the ill use of the Sweet Gift of Bacchus, he has the curiosity to slink up to the roof of his College where 'by a piece of unwarrantable boldness I got a sight of Madam Venus in her transit, through the College Telescope. You must know that the College had not long ago a present of a Telescope, but that whatever belongs to the college . . . belongs only to the fellows . . . so that we had no hopes of seeing this remarkable Phænomenon which it was allmost impossible we should ever have an Opportunity of seeing again in our lives . . . but I and two others . . . at about ¼ after 6 stole up the common-room stairs and marched up to the leads where the fellows had brought the Telescope for the convenience of observing the Phænomenon. . . . However we got a sight of it at last' . . . and so forth, asking incidentally 'whether there was any Satellite that attended Venus in her passage over the Sun, as some of our people thought they saw one . . .' Always an unresting intelligence and unwavering affection go hand in hand: to his father again, 'the best Testimony I can give you of my gratitude I have given by accompanying this with 20 pages of Tully . . .'. As at length he reaches the end of those rather tiresome Tusculan disputations he concludes:

> 'My duty to my Grandmama and love to my dear Brother;
> Accipe quos mitto, studii, Pater optime, fructus;
> En tibi longi operis, denique finis adest.'

In 1763 he is admitted to Lincoln's Inn and begins his law studies. Four years later we find him attending scientific lectures by the Professor of Astronomy at Oxford. In 1769 he is admitted to the Bar. In 1772 he is working on an analysis of offences and punishments and is preparing his *Introduction to the Principles of Morals and Legislation*. Whatever he is doing, whomever he meets or desires to meet—extending recurrently to Catherine the Great of Russia to whom he wishes to present his work on Punishments as a means of reforming the Russian code—is reflected vividly in his unceasing correspondence. For the moment, pending a third volume of letters, we may leave him in active interchange with his adored younger brother Samuel who had been trained as a shipwright or naval architect and in 1780 travelled to Russia in search (ultimately successful) of employment in the service of the Empress. This fitted in with, and was no doubt partly prompted by, Jeremy's ambition to implant his 'Code' and 'Punishments' in the Russian Empress's mind; to which end he was busily attempting to secure the translation of the Introduction of his Code into German, as a means of publicizing it. All this is the subject of a detailed correspondence with Samuel in St. Petersburg, but does not prevent him from including or enclosing detailed notes on the sheathing of nuts on the Perseus or the loss of rudders hung by a 'patent Metal' instead of iron on four ships-of-war anchored in Torbay during a gale.

These and many others are of course merely little byways in the vast landscape of a universal mind—the sort of revealing discursions which are apt to the idiom of epistolary conversation. In a multitude of ways, equally important or unconsidered, these letters present from moment to moment the curiosity of a restless polymath who, in nearly consecutive sentences, can express a very genuine anxiety as to his poor dear brother Sammy's sickness, the satisfaction at having bought a Spinnet 'as I could have one very cheap', and astonishment at the conversion of some of his Oxford friends to the 'Methodistical doctrine', transforming them into 'Fanaticks that are much more Enthusiastical than the Methodists of London' so that they no longer 'take a tune upon the Fiddle together'. Here from page to page is not merely a living mind but a living social scene. In other words it is an aperitif for the substantial meal which is to follow.

Looking forward, that meal is to include shortly the *Introduction to the Principles of Morals and Legislation*, under the editorship of Professors J. H. Burns and H. L. A. Hart, and a new edition of the text originally published by Professor Everett as the *Limits of Jurisprudence Defined* which now will appear with substantial changes under the title *Of Laws in General*, also edited by Professor Hart. A further volume of correspondence—by no means the last —edited by Professor Christie, is well advanced. Work too has already begun on Bentham's *Constitutional Code*, his writings on Religion and the Church, his *Theory of Punishment*, and his *Deontology*; and a number of other volumes, among them an edition of Bentham's logical writings by Professor Hart, are in the exploratory stage.

It is thus hoped that justice will at last be done to all the products of Jeremy Bentham's versatile pen and that students of a future age will be able to utilize to the full his works in all the fields he cultivated.

(viii) EARLY ENGLISH CHURCH MUSIC

For many years prior to the period under review, the Academy had taken an active interest, without administrative responsibility, in the collection and publication of *Monumenta Musicae Byzantinae*, a flourishing project of the Union Académique Internationale. It had, however, no specific niche in its own organization for musical enterprises of the kind, nor indeed for art-history as a whole, although it had an endowed lectureship on Aspects of Art, and from time to time touched upon the fine arts in other contexts. The position was regularized at the end of 1950, when Section XI (History of Art) hived off from Section X (Archaeology) and was designed to include the history of music amongst its studies.

Accordingly, when in 1961 a new musical project of considerable dimensions was mooted, it had an academic home to go to. It originated in Oxford, and Dr. W. F. Oakeshott, Rector of Lincoln College, took it up tentatively in first instance with the Academy's Secretary. It had already been discussed and partially developed under the primary leadership of Dr. E. J. Wellesz, with the support of Dr. F. Ll. Harrrison and Professor Sir Jack Westrup; and an approach had been made to the Pilgrim Trust for the necessary initial funds. Would the Academy now take the whole project under its wing?

Encouraging, though necessarily provisional, interchanges took place in the autumn between the Secretary and the President of the Academy, the Pilgrim Trust, and the Oxford group; and at its November Meeting the Council of the Academy warmly welcomed the proposal. A mixed Committee of Academicians and non-Academicians was set up, consisting of Sir Jack Westrup, F.B.A. (Chairman), Professor Henry Chadwick, F.B.A., Dr. E. H. J. Gombrich, F.B.A., Dr. F. Ll. Harrison, and Professor A. C. Lewis;[1] and at its first meeting, on 16 December 1961, the nature, object, administration, and plans of the newly initiated scheme were reviewed. The following report and decisions were recorded:

[1] Dr. Walter Oakeshott was added in 1964 and Dr. E. J. Wellesz, F.B.A., in 1965.

1. The nature of the project: to produce a series of octavo publications of polyphonic English Church Music down to *c.* 1640.

2. The object of the project: to make available editions which are both scholarly and practical.

3. Administration: in support of this scheme the Pilgrim Trust had already deposited with the British Academy the sum of £6,100, of which £2,600 were an outright gift to cover editorial expenses for a year, while £3,500 were a loan, repayable at the Academy's convenience from sales, to subsidize publishing costs until the volumes should be self-supporting.

The series would be published for the Academy by the experienced firm of Stainer and Bell, in accordance with an agreement (already signed) between the Academy and Dr. F. Ll. Harrison as the general editor and administrator of the project under the Committee; and copyright would be held by the Academy. Another agreement, between the Academy and Stainer & Bell concurring details of copyright, royalty, etc., was ready for signature after scrutiny by the Committee and the Academy. (This agreement, after revision, was signed on 23 May 1962.) Accounts would be audited by the Academy.

The bulk of the editing would fall upon Dr. J. D. Bergsagel, 'a very able young Canadian scholar' (Oakeshott) with a special interest in early Tudor and pre-Tudor music, who would be full-time paid Executive Editor under the Committee. He would be assisted by editors of individual volumes who would be paid a fee to be decided by the Committee, varying in relation to the size of the volume edited and the nature of the editorial work, but not to exceed £75. This fee would be supplemented by a royalty payment after the volume had paid its publishing costs. The General Editor (Dr. Harrison) would receive 10 per cent of the proceeds of sales.

4. Plans: the first four volumes were already firmly planned. In fact the volumes as published, with dates, down to 1969 have been:

  i. *Early Tudor Masses* I (Festal Masses; Richard Alwood, Thomas Ashewell), transcribed and edited by Bergsagel, 1963.
  ii. *William Mundy: Latin Antiphons and Psalms*, transcribed and edited by F. Ll. Harrison, 1963.
  iii. *Orlando Gibbons: Verse Anthems*, transcribed and edited by David Wulstan, 1964.
  iv. *Early Tudor Magnificats* I, transcribed and edited by Paul Doe, 1964.

v.   *Thomas Tomkins: Musica Deo Sacra* I, transcribed and edited by
     Bernard Rose, 1964.
vi. *Early Tudor Organ Music I: Music for the Office*, transcribed and
     edited by John Caldwell, 1966.
vii. *Robert Ramsey I: English Sacred Music*, transcribed and edited by
     Edward Thompson, 1967.
viii. *Fifteenth-century Liturgical Music I: Antiphons and Music for Holy
     Week and Easter*, transcribed and edited by Andrew Hughes,
     1968.
ix. *Thomas Tomkins: Musica Deo Sacra* II, transcribed and edited by
     Bernard Rose, 1968.
x.   *Early Tudor Organ Music II: Music for the Mass*, transcribed and
     edited by Denis Stevens, 1969.

Problems of finance were not absent from this project but were
greatly alleviated by the continuing liberality of the Pilgrim
Trustees. Their two initial grants have been recorded above: an
outright gift for editorial expenses and a loan towards the primary
costs of printing and publication. By July 1962 it was clear that
delays in printing would defer the production (and resulting profits)
of Volume I beyond the anticipated date, and, on the intervention of Dr. Oakeshott, the Trust generously renewed the grant
of £2,600 for 1962–3, at the same time asking for a detailed programme of future publications. When the Committee's schedule
reached the Academy in March 1963, it was found to envisage
the expenditure of nearly £14,000 on editorial activities during
the next five-year period. An accompanying letter from Dr. Oakeshott (himself a Pilgrim Trustee) described this as a 'formidable
proposition', unlikely perhaps to commend itself to his colleagues.
Would the Academy ease the impact by underwriting half of the
estimated sum, i.e. to an amount of about £1,500 a year?

Briefly, at its May meeting the Council of the Academy accepted this proposal, and expressed to the Pilgrim Trustees the
hope that they might feel moved to contribute an equivalent
amount, thus completing the total sum required. Shortly afterwards Dr. Oakeshott was able to tell his fellow-Trustees that he
was trying elsewhere to secure contributions towards the sum
required from them, and decision on their part was accordingly
postponed.

In October the Trust heard from Dr. Oakeshott that he had,
for each of the five years now in question, obtained from All Souls
College an annual grant of £250 and a similar sum from the Elm-
grant Trust. These two benefactions left a minimum deficit of
£840 on the £1,500 (or rather less) still required. The Pilgrim

Trust very handsomely weighed in with this sum, and the needed total was attained. Meanwhile the preparation of new volumes proceeded, as has been shown, at a commendable speed, and so continues. The proved value of the scheme and the tireless production of its contributory scholars may, it is to be hoped, continue to outweigh the administrative difficulties which from time to time attend its enthusiastic progress.

(ix) COMPUTERS IN TEXTUAL CRITICISM

> He settled *Hoti's* business—let it be!—
> Properly based *Oun*—
> Gave us the doctrine of the enclitic *De,*
> Dead from the waist down.

Today for that sort of business, as for much else, we are being taught to turn our problems into the computer, and the subtleties of textual criticism are no exception. Indeed, if we are content with linguistic niceties and authenticities, it may contribute to our comfort to reflect that the omniscient machine can read the New Testament in three and a half minutes or the complete epics of Homer in five minutes; or even, as the Revd. A. Q. Morton, thus fortified, was able to assure us half a dozen years ago, can demonstrate that only four of the fourteen epistles of St. Paul are from the same mind or hand.

Accordingly, in February 1966 it seemed fitting and normal that the Secretary of the Academy should address the following note to Professor E. G. Turner as a percipient man of words and Chairman of Section V (Classical Literature and Philology): 'The Council agreed to the proposal that a small committee should be set up to deal with aspects of the use of computers in relation to textual analysis, and we should be very glad if you would accept—at any rate for the time being—the Chairmanship of the Committee. Your fellow members are Professor R. G. D. (Sir Roy) Allen, Professor (Dame) Helen Gardner, Mr. C. H. Roberts and Mr. T. C. Skeat.' Professor Turner accepted with the reservation that Professor K. J. Dover of St. Andrews, who was expected to (and in fact shortly did) become a Fellow of the Academy, was the right man for the job and should be co-opted forthwith.

Thereafter followed a period of exploration and discussion which can now be left to the obscurity of the files. Several universities, including Edinburgh, Glasgow, and Leeds, were interested, as were a number of individual scholars, but in a new kind of enterprise involving special skills and machinery there was, quite naturally, a hint perhaps of competition rather than of co-ordination, and advance was slow and devious. Were there questions of copyright, and if so what? Was it desirable to establish a library of computer tapes and what was required to make it function? And in what centre? Who would be responsible for maintenance, loans, acquisitions? e.g. a junior member of a university academic staff? or an assistant librarian in a library? and for exchange of tapes, etc.? How was the relevant money to be handled? (Obviously this must be under the control of the Academy, which would no doubt be expected to supply funds at least in part from its Research Fund.) And so on. Rather than display the tangle of argument which enwrapped these and other problems, it is preferable here to proceed direct to the solutions which ultimately (in 1968) secured provisional agreement. They were these, as drafted by Professor Dover, who had meanwhile assumed the Chairmanship of the project:

1. The Committee on the Use of Computers in Textual Criticism proposes a scheme of collaboration between the Academy and the Department of Computer Science in the University of Edinburgh.

2. At present the initiative for the compilation of word-indexes and for the retrieval of information from texts on tape comes from individuals who know what they themselves would like to have available, know what computers are useful for this type of work, and have reason to think that they can get grants of money for the purpose. There has been no systematic attempt to arrange work in any order of priority. The Sections of the Academy seem to be the appropriate bodies to decide on priorities and to initiate work, and it is suggested that Sections concerned with languages and literature should be asked each year to say what they would regard as most helpful to the advancement of their subjects.

3. It is also suggested that the Sections concerned should define the standards of refinement which should be observed in the transcription of any given language on to tape—defining, for example, the extent to which vowel-quantity should be shown in Latin, or stress-accent in Slavonic languages. It should be borne in mind that the discovery of phonemic and rhythmical patterns is a task for which computers are peculiarly suitable.

4. It is further suggested that at this stage no account should be taken of the mechanical limitations of teleprinters or of the

difficulty of finding adequately trained operators. The important thing is that scholars should state what is desirable; if they will do this, the next stage will be to discover how far what is desirable is also practicable.

5. It is highly desirable to establish international standards. As a step in this direction it was hoped that Professor Dover might confer with Professor R. R. Dyer, of the University of Indiana, who has experience of computational work in the U.S.A. on the text of Homer.

In July 1968 the Secretary of the Academy made a formal approach to the Principal of the University of Edinburgh in the following terms:

Dear Principal,

The British Academy has recently set up a Committee on the use of computers for the analysis of literary texts under the Chairmanship of Professor K. J. Dover, F.B.A., of St. Andrews. Applications for grants for the production of literary tapes are now coming in, and it is proposed also to initiate some computational projects.

Our immediate problem is to find a skilled agent in this matter, and we have consulted Professor S. Michaelson informally about the problem. Professor Michaelson is both interested and experienced in work of this kind, and he has welcomed a proposal that the British Academy should offer the execution of its projects to his Edinburgh Department of Computer Science. The Academy would pay the salary of a part-time librarian who would be responsible, in that Department, for the custody and cataloguing of literary tapes and for dealing in first instance with correspondence relating to requests for copies and other relevant matters.

For this part-time librarianship Professor Michaelson suggests the appointment of the Rev. A. Q. Morton, with whom he has collaborated closely for some time. We approve of this proposal ... Professor Michaelson would remain in close contact with his work and Professor Dover would be available for consultation.

I accordingly write to ask if you would be willing to appoint Mr. Morton as part-time librarian in your Department of Computer Science, on the understanding that the Academy will pay (the agreed costs, amounting to £400). The Academy hopes that by 'adopting' in this fashion a single computer department as the executive agent in all matters relating to the production of literary tapes it may avert the wasteful multiplication of labour which is liable to accrue unless the closest co-operation can be assured.

We should be most grateful if you would consent to give this proposal a sympathetic thought ...

To this, Dr. Michael Swann, the Principal, replied (18 July 1968): '. . . I can say that we should be glad to help and to fall in with your suggestions . . .' The agreement with the Academy was to be for three years in the first instance, and Mr. Morton was duly appointed as part-time librarian. It was now the spring of 1969, and the Computer Committee, satisfactorily organized and ready for work, passes beyond the purview of the present record. Its first projects included the completion of the taping of certain texts published in the *Oxyrhynchus Papyri* and the initiation of the taping of Apollonius Rhodius.

XII

MONOGRAPHS AND SERIES

As an addendum to the last chapter it is proper and useful to assemble a miscellaneous collection of Academy projects ranging from the publication of isolated monographs on a more or less adventitious basis to serial publications issued or instituted under sustained general schemes during the two decades now in question. Of the former it is sufficient here to print a list, in which the individual items have little or no linkage beyond their common contribution to some aspect of humanistic scholarship. Briefly they are as follows:

W. W. Greg, *Jonson's 'Masque of Gipsies' in the Burley, Belvoir, and Windsor Versions: an attempt at Reconstruction.* 1952.

Cyril Fox, *Offa's Dyke: a Field Survey of the Western Frontier-works of Mercia in the Seventh and Eighth Centuries A.D.* 1955. A collection and revision of a series of partial surveys previously published piecemeal but worthy of comprehensive treatment; a masterly recension of a major historico-archaeological problem.

A. E. Popham, *Correggio's Drawings.* 1957. A definitive study of the material by a former Keeper of Prints and Drawings at the British Museum.

Evelyn Jamison, *Admiral Eugenius of Sicily: His Life and Works.* 1957.

Elisabeth Rosenbaum, *Cyrenaican Portrait Sculpture.* 1960. A collection of sculpture from a major Graeco-Roman city in North Africa.

Mortimer Wheeler, *Charsada: A Metropolis of the North-West Frontier.* 1962. Report of an excavation carried out jointly by the Academy and the Pakistan Government on the site of the former capital of Gandhara on the Peshawar plain.

Jale Inan and Elisabeth Rosenbaum, *Roman and Early Byzantine Portrait Sculpture in Asia Minor.* 1966. An annotated collection otherwise largely unknown.

David Oates, *Studies in the Ancient History of Northern Iraq.* 1968. Inspired by, but extending far beyond, pioneer work carried out by Sir Aurel Stein in 1938–9.

J. M. de Navarro, *The Finds from the Site of La Tène*: Volume I (two parts), *Scabbards and the Swords found in them.* (In the press).

G. P. Cuttino, *Gascon Register A (Series of 1318–1319)*, edited from British Museum Cottonian MS. Julius E.1, with the collaboration of J.-P. Trabut-Cussec. 3 volumes. A definitive edition, the work of many years, of a mixed collection of manuscripts relating to the affairs of

Gascony and the dukedom of Aquitaine in the times of Henry III and Edward I and II of England. Towards the considerable costs of this publication a grant of 9,000 dollars (£3,208) has been received from the John Simon Guggenheim Memorial Foundation. (In the press).

Of the volumes published in series, the well-known Schweich Lectures on Biblical Archaeology constitute the longest run, going back as they do to 1908. During the period now in question, three have been issued:

Roland de Vaux, *L'Archéologie et les Manuscrits de la Mer Morte*. 1959.
Kathleen M. Kenyon, *Amorites and Canaanites*. 1963.
Edward Ullendorff, *Ethiopia and the Bible*. 1967.

More recent series, originating within the past ten years, call for fuller introduction. The first is a new series of medieval Latin texts, and is known formally as *Auctores Britannici Medii Aevi*. It was inaugurated in 1959 on the recommendation of Section II, which appointed a Sectional Committee to shape the project. Its aim was to secure the publication of medieval texts dealing with intellectual subjects—theological and philosophical thought and learning, political theory and so forth—for which there was at present no provision in this country. Council approved, and set up an Editorial Committee consisting of Professor M. D. Knowles (Chairman), Professor E. F. Jacob, and Dr. W. A. Pantin; Dr. R. W. Hunt was later added.

At the outset, two volumes of this new series were said to be practically ready for the press, but Professor Knowles, who had worked hard upon the scheme in all its administrative details, was still, in September 1963, 'extremely disappointed' that the volumes 'always disappeared from sight just before they got to delivery'. Details of this sad story need not be disinterred, but in fact it was not until January 1965 that the semi-final text of *Memorials of Saint Anselm*, edited by R. W. Southern and F. S. Schmitt, O.S.B., reached the Academy, and only a year or more later could it claim completeness. The subsequent transit through the Press was a prolonged operation, and in fact the volume did not see the light of day until July 1969. In spite, or because, of its retarded birth it was a bonny child, first of what may be hoped to be a noble line. Meanwhile, in January 1967, the second volume in the series—the earliest philosophical work of an Oxford master (thirteenth century), *John Blund: Tractatus de Anima*, edited mainly by Dr. D. A. Callus but completed after his death by Dr. R. W. Hunt—was sent to the Press where, at the time of writing, it remains. It is only fair, for the appeasement of the impatient layman, to emphasize that the editing and printing of these often very exigent texts is a task 'Ohne Hast, aber ohne Rast'. Other volumes are in preparation.

From medieval texts to Anglo-Saxon graves and graveyards. These will not, alas, detain us long. Nevertheless, in its inception the scheme for a *Corpus of Anglo-Saxon Graves and Grave-goods* had everything to commend it. The first move took the form of a convincing proposal submitted in February 1959 by Professor C. F. C. Hawkes and Mrs. Sonia Hawkes to Section X (Archaeology), in the following terms:

The Anglo-Saxon settlements in England can be studied by archaeology wherever they have left graves showing burial in the heathen mode —which required for cremations normally at least an urn and wherever possible, as inhumations chiefly show, personal belongings bestowed as grave-goods. The historical value of this study is now well appreciated; and when new cemeteries of such graves are found, they seldom escape due archaeological attention. But the great bulk of Anglo-Saxon grave-goods extant, naturally, is what has accrued from past discovery, conserved up and down the country in museums. And this, taken as a whole, is worse represented in our published literature than any comparable class of the national antiquities. Through that deficiency, excavators of fresh sites are hampered, by the difficulty of comparison, in appraising their finds correctly, and students of the period, when confronted with individual interpretations, often cannot test them by referring to the relevant material. . . . We submit, then, that the time is now fully ripe for the initiation of a Corpus of Anglo-Saxon Graves and Grave-goods, in a series of uniform volumes, with the ultimate aim of comprehending the entire material. We ask the Academy to accept, in principle, that this plan is just, and moreover that it should itself, as the national body pre-eminently suited to such enterprises, undertake to publish the work in its own name. We offer ourselves as Editors, and are ready to bear responsibility for controlling both the priorities of choice of subject-matter, and the uniformities of textual and graphic presentation . . . We believe that the beginning should be made among the early cemeteries of Kent. . . .

This project, after further correspondence, was passed on to Council, which accepted it in 1960 and allotted £400 towards the initial costs, with further sums from year to year. In 1965 Council, on the representation of Section X, appointed an 'Anglo-Saxon Graves and Grave-goods Committee' under the Chairmanship of Dr. J. N. L. Myres to ease the path of progress. Assets in the form of drawings and annotations accumulated behind the scenes at a modest pace, but illness most regrettably intervened. In his

Progress Report for 1968, **Dr.** Myres could only assure Council that 'Work has proceeded on the lines agreed between the Committee and the Editors in December 1966 . . .'; and for the time being we must reluctantly be content to echo G. K. Chesterton's solemn words:

'And they that rule in England,
  In stately conclave met,
Alas, alas for England
  They have no graves as yet.'

Now for *Anglo-Saxon Charters*. These were still mere seedlings at the end of the period now under review. It will suffice here to record that in July 1966 a Committee set up jointly by the Academy and the Royal Historical Society met at the Institute of Historical Research to consider the publication by the Academy of a substantive edition of the Anglo-Saxon Charters. The main lines of the proposed work were laid down and a report was submitted at length to the Academy's Section II (Medieval and Modern History) in January 1967. Rarely can any Section of the Academy have been confronted with so formidable a body of documentation. To say that this comprised both a Majority and a Minority Report, both equally and ardently in favour of the general proposal, and that its authors included essays or exclamations from Professor H. P. R. Finberg, Professor V. H. Galbraith, Dr. P. Chaplais, Dr. Florence Harmer, Professor Dorothy Whitelock, and Sir Goronwy Edwards, is to emphasize regret that repetition is not here feasible. Suffice it that Council was in no mood to question the validity of the recommendation, and that the Joint Committee promptly got to work on three fascicules or volumes: Professor A. Campbell agreed to edit the Rochester Charters, Dr. P. Chaplais those of Exeter and other south-western houses, and Mr. P. H. Sawyer (who is incidentally Secretary of the Committee) those of Burton Abbey. It is hoped that all of these will be ready for the Committee by the end of 1970, and that by then editors for further fascicules will have been appointed. At the same time a collection of photographs is being built up, with the help of a grant from the Academy, for the use of editors and for possible facsimile publication.

Last in this list is a project put forward in January 1966 by the philosophers, Section VII, in response to a memorandum circulated by the Secretary inviting Sections to devise new research-schemes in the light of the gradually increasing viability of the Academy's research funds. The reaction of Section VII to this appeal was that, while co-operative philosophical research was not likely to gain directly by the organized efforts of the Academy, there was, on the other hand, a great need for new editors and translators of the works of many of the great philosophers. There was, moreover, some impressive evidence that bad and in some cases grossly incompetent translations had recently been published, and the existence of these might deter publishers from taking on the responsibility of providing respectable translations and editors. The Section expressed the view that two steps might usefully be taken by the Academy: (i) Respectable British publishers might be notified by the Academy that funds were available for subsidising work of this kind under editors or translators who were likely to meet the high standards required. (ii) Members of the Section and also of other interested Sections (e.g. Section V) might be sent notices asking them to inform the Academy if they themselves were interested in or knew of others proposing to undertake work of this kind.

On the strength of this recommendation, Council set up a *Classical and Medieval Logic Texts Committee*, comprising Professor W. C. Kneale (Chairman), Mr. A. N. Prior, Professor P. T. Geach, and Dr. L. Minio-Paluello. This Committee, meeting at Oxford in February 1967, recommended that in first instance works of three categories should be translated:

(a) Text books used in medieval universities: e.g. Boethius's logical treatises, perhaps with some selections from his commentaries on Aristotle; Priscian (in selections).

(b) Developed logical treatises: e.g. Albert of Saxony's *Perutilis logica*.

(c) Philosophical works, not themselves logical treatises, but of high logical interest: e.g. Buridan's commentary on the *Physics*.

Under (c) Professor Geach was invited to discuss with Mr. Roger White and Mr. Timothy Potts of the University of Leeds a scheme for the translation of Anselm's three dialogues, *De veritate*, *De libero arbitrio*, and *De casu diaboli*. (Since the Medieval Texts Committee was already concerned with Anselm, the Secretary of the Academy was at pains to ascertain that there was no unnecessary overlap between the Committees. Professor Knowles reassured him but agreed that there should be a specific liaison between the two bodies to avoid duplication and to pool knowledge of possible texts. Professor Kneale was likewise of the opinion that the aims of the two projects were essentially different.)

On this general basis, the Committee for Classical and Medieval Logic Texts finally focussed its attention in 1969 upon the preparation of an edition of Part I of Paul of Venice's *Logica Magna* and assembled a formidable band of Editors for the purpose. They include Professor Norman Kretzmann of Cornell, Professor Geach (General Editor), Dr. D. P. Henry of Manchester, Dr. T. C. Potts of Leeds, Professor R. G. Wengert of Illinois at Urbana, and Dr. C. Williams of Bristol. A grant from the Academy enabled each editor to have a complete photostat of the early printed text and a copy of the Vatican Manuscript with which it is to be collated. The outcome is awaited.

XIII

FOREIGN EXCHANGES AND DOMESTIC PARTNERSHIP

I N its first fifty years the British Academy was essentially a passive *corps d'élite*. During the subsequent twenty years it gradually woke to action as a prop and stimulant to research, by materially encouraging British Schools or Institutes abroad and by adding to their number, by fostering new work and publication with the aid of benevolent Foundations, by extending its scope generally, and by creating in the minds of British scholarship and not least in those of Whitehall the increasing conviction that it was becoming an active and useful impulse and was more than an honourable refuge for achievement. Ultimately, in 1962, this new urge found expression, as has been shown, in the Rockefeller Report and its sequel, Government's explicit recognition of humanistic research as an official commitment.

But if the Academy was achieving something of a new status at home, its standing amongst the learned institutions of the world at large was still very inadequate. In part this was due, no doubt, to the circumstances from which it sprang. Aside from the exceptional and well-understood fragmentation of the French Academy, rooted in long processes of cultural evolution, it is normal for foreign Academies to comprise both the Humanities and the Natural Sciences. Such in part was the intent of the Royal Society of London for Improving Natural Knowledge from its inception in 1660-2. Long afterwards its *Philosophical Transactions* continued to include, alongside widely ranging enquiries into natural phenomena, accounts of Roman altars, pavements, hypocausts, pottery and wall-paintings, Greek and Roman coins, ancient camps, and even Sanskrit manuscripts. But from the first it was dominated by the problems and curiosities of the natural rather than the historical world; and the burgeoning of natural science in the nineteenth century meant the increasing exclusion of dissertations upon human artifacts. These were now for the most part relegated to the Society of Antiquaries of London, the second-oldest of our British learned sodalities, only forty-five years younger than the Royal itself. For long the two bodies did not resist a measure of functional overlap. From 1707 to

1846 all save one of the Presidents of the Antiquaries were also Fellows of the Royal Society. But in the twentieth century only three out of fifteen P.S.A.'s have shared the honours. The cleavage between Nature and Art had appeared to be almost complete.

The first formal and public demonstration of this dichotomy was the expressed inability of the Royal Society at Wiesbaden in 1899 to represent the Humanities. In more general terms it may later be said to have inspired C. P. Snow's familiar affirmation of 'The Two Cultures' in his Rede Lecture at Cambridge in 1959; 'literary intellectuals at one pole—at the other scientists. Between the two a gulf of mutual incomprehension'. Elsewhere I have disputed the continuing validity of this somewhat archaic view. It ignores, or insufficiently comprehends, a steadily increasing interchange between the sciences and the humanities—an interchange which has been important since the end of the eighteenth century and has become of vital value during the past quarter-century. Many of the ideas and techniques inherent in the basic study of man are rooted in scientific disciplines, and even literary analysis and criticism are learning to depend more and more upon the machinery and technology of science. It might be claimed, with an appreciable degree of truth, that the continuing separation of the functions of the Royal Society and the Academy is schizophrenic rather than rational, and is sustained in practice only by one overriding factor: that of the sheer unwieldiness of the material bulk involved. If natural sciences have proliferated, so have the humanities. There is no longer room for them all together in one old lady's shoe. The best that can be hoped is that the pair of shoes may march conformably.

For several years after 1949 these problems of function and status, both at home and abroad, were necessarily subordinated to the primary task of building up the immediate resources of the Academy from next-to-nothing to something like a respectable competence. But they were not absent from our minds. In 1945, for example, the Trustees of the Sir Halley Stewart Trust had been good enough to make a grant of £500 to the Academy, through its President, Sir John Clapham, for the purpose of bringing to this country distinguished men of learning from the Continent in order that they might again make contact with learned circles in Great Britain in the difficult period after the war. Preference was at first given to scholars from Holland and Belgium, but the scope was later widened to include other countries, and the scheme, relatively small, proved of appreciable service.

As the result also of recommendations made by a sub-committee appointed by the Council of the Academy, a useful mission was undertaken by Sir Harold Bell and Sir Charles Webster in 1946 to Berlin, Göttingen, and Bonn with a view also to re-establishing relations with Germany in the humanistic field. It was natural, therefore, that in the 'Webster Period' thoughts should again be turned to developing and enlarging the Academy's overseas contacts and responsibilities. As an index of this thinking, it may here be recorded that Charles Webster left to the Academy a residuary bequest (happily not yet available) to facilitate the participation of Fellows of the Academy in overseas projects, including representation at the international conferences which were always near to his heart. Later with the ready help of the British Council attempts, partially successful, were made to organize scholarly exchanges with the U.S.S.R., Hungary, and Bulgaria; these may be noted here as tentative small-scale beginnings rather than as substantive achievements.

First the U.S.S.R. At the end of 1959 an Agreement was signed between the Governments of the U.K. and the U.S.S.R. on relations in the scientific, technical, educational, and cultural fields during 1960–1. The Academy was included within this Agreement under the recommendation that 'during the said period the Academy of Sciences of the Union of Soviet Socialist Republics and the British Academy will effect an exchange of two Soviet and two British philosophers for a period of two weeks'. On the suggestion of the British Council, which was to bear the appropriate costs of this modest exchange, the President of the British Academy wrote to the President of the Academy of Sciences of the U.S.S.R. welcoming the proposal and suggesting dates. Months passed without reply, although the British Council activated our Ambassador in Moscow. A later note in the file suggests the possible reason: 'the Russians would deal with only one body in this country, namely the Royal Society, since though their own Academy covers both the sciences and the humanities they are interested primarily in the sciences'. Is the H-bomb less dangerous than ideas? Anyway, subsequent Cultural Agreements with the U.S.S.R. retain the primacy of science but empower the British Council 'and other appropriate organizations of the United Kingdom' to exchange specialists in fields other than the natural sciences. It remains to be seen how this arrangement works in practice. Throughout the frustrate negotiations of the past decade, which were more extended than is here indicated and included well-meant intervention by the Society for Cultural Relations with the U.S.S.R., the British Council did everything posssible to secure success.

Better fortune attended negotiations carried out in 1962 by the United Kingdom, represented by the Foreign Office and the British Council, with the Hungarian People's Republic, whereby both sides agreed to encourage the development of contacts between the Royal Society and the British Academy on the one hand and the Hungarian Academy of Sciences on the other. Expenses would be shared between the British Council and the Hungarian authorities, and the duration of each visit would normally be a fortnight. Interchanges proceeded at some length between the British Academy, in consultation with the British Council, and the Hungarian Academy of Sciences; and it was eventually agreed that Dr. J. J. Wilkes, Research Fellow in the Department of Latin at the University of Birmingham and a specialist in the history and archaeology of the Balkan provinces of the Roman Empire, and Professor J. N. Findlay, F.B.A., University Professor of Philosophy at King's College, London, should visit Hungary for approximately two weeks under the Academy's auspices, respectively in May 1963 and January 1964.

The scheme began to show promise of continuing success under renewed Agreements of the same kind. Unhappily exchange in the fields of humanistic scholarship was limited (by finance) to one candidate in each year, and a number of suitable applicants were thereby discouraged. In the event, the next British visitor did not get away to Hungary until October 1966, when Mr. J. W. Pope-Hennessy, F.B.A., Director of the Victoria and Albert Museum, was able to pay a somewhat hurried but profitable visit to Budapest. There he was met by Professor László Mátrai on behalf of the Hungarian Academy and was intelligently entertained. In return, Dr. Mátrai—Director of the University Library at Budapest and a student of philosophy and social science—visited the U.K. in February–March 1967 to fulfil a busy round of engagements in London and Oxford (including one to the Covent Garden Ballet as the guest of Lord Robbins), and was everywhere a welcome and appreciative guest.

Other exchanges followed. On our side competition for the one annual place has complicated rather than simplified problems of time-table. But in the summer of 1968 Dr. Christopher Hill, F.B.A., Master of Balliol, was happily received in Budapest by the infallible Dr. Mátrai, and on the other side Professor G. Eörsi, Corresponding Fellow of the Hungarian Academy of

Sciences and Professor of Civil Law in the Eötvös Loránd University of Budapest, was suitably entertained in London and Oxford in March 1969. Further exchanges have been arranged more recently, and there is no doubt that an enlargement of the present meagre provision would be generally acceptable.

Parallel with the Hungarian exchanges, talks in Sofia in May 1965 produced a similar programme of cultural, educational, scientific, and technological exchanges between the United Kingdom and the People's Republic of Bulgaria for 1965–7: an agreement subsequently renewed biennially. The named intermediaries were again the British Council, the Royal Society, and the British Academy on the U.K. side, with the Bulgarian Academy of Sciences and the Bulgarian Academy of Agricultural Sciences on the other. Details may be left to the files, but it is of interest to record here that, as in the case of Hungary, there has been no lack of competition for the single humanistic vacancy annually available. The normal duration of each visit is again a fortnight. Within reach of the period now under review, Mr. A. J. P. Taylor, F.B.A., headed the list for 1967–8 (for the specific purpose of seeing Orthodox monasteries and modern historians), and was followed by Dr. C. A. Macartney, F.B.A., in 1968–9 and Mr. E. S. Higgs of the Cambridge Department of Archaeology in 1969–70. Mr. Higgs, as Director of the 'Early History of Agriculture' Project sponsored by the Academy and the University of Cambridge, was anxious to make contact with the Institute of Archaeology in Sofia and to meet members of the Bulgarian Academy of Sciences interested in the application of scientific techniques to archaeological data, particularly in zoology and botany. Other applicants await their turn.

These occasional visits and courtesies arranged under diplomatic agreement and nursed (most amiably) by the British Council were welcomed as gestures but did not seriously enlarge the international machinery of scholarship. Perhaps in natural science even more than the humanities, some far more systematic interchange of skills and problems is today a crying need of advancing scholarship, and technology. It was appropriate that the Royal Society, with its tremendous prestige and experience and, no doubt, its resources, should lead the way. No less happily, on 16 February 1968 its urge for new action directed the footsteps of Sir Harold Thompson, F.R.S., and Dr. David Martin, respectively Foreign Secretary and Executive Secretary of the Royal Society, to the rooms of the British Academy where the President (Sir Kenneth Wheare) and the Secretary awaited them. The subsequent discussion, fortified thereafter by impressive documentation, did more than bare the bones of the very considerable problem of effective international exchange; it also made very clear the need for close and sensible collaboration between the Royal Society and the British Academy in giving that problem an organic viability. As has been recalled above, the duality of the British system, with its two independent embodiments of what was on the Continent normally a single comprehensive corpus of learning, was a constant source of puzzlement to our Continental colleagues and of entanglement in mutual negotiation. This was incidentally emphasized with some regret by a useful meeting of fifteen representatives of European academies held at the Royal Society in October 1968 under the chairmanship of Sir Harold Thompson and, by invitation, attended by the Secretary of the British Academy. In discussion, the Secretary took the opportunity of explaining to our foreign visitors the history of this dual system, admitting that it was now increasingly difficult to maintain the dividing line in subjects such as geography, anthropology, and archaeology, and that there were today indeed very close links in many disciplines between what used to be known as the sciences and the humanities. The British Academy was well aware of these problems and looked forward to a closer co-operation in the provision for a regular interchange of scholars, not only between centres of learning in Europe but also with those of India, Pakistan, Persia, and the Further East.

The meeting just cited was a stock-taking of a European Science Exchange Programme which had originated at a conference of representatives of Academies and equivalent organizations from twelve European countries held at the Royal Society in December 1966. The humanities were not yet involved in this programme, and the British Academy was not therefore a party to it. But for the record a brief summary of its nature and progress is desirable at this point in the light of present and future developments.

The Royal Society had been able to obtain for this exchange-project from private sources about £40,000 a year for each of the years 1967 to 1969. Accordingly, in January 1967 it started the programme by circularizing its Fellows and appropriate institutions in the U.K. inviting applications for fellowships, short-term study visits, and assistance for small specialized research conferences. The response was immediate and encouraging; so much so that at a second meeting of European representatives at the Deutsche Forschungsgemeinschaft in Bad Godesberg in April 1967 it was shown that the funds available to the Royal Society were insufficient to meet the quantity and the quality of the applications.

According steps were taken to establish a 'balancing' mechanism by which the Royal Society agreed—using funds promised from the Department of Education and Science—to match sums made available by organizations of other countries: a plan which incidentally eliminated the major problems of currency transfer. Similar 'balancing' funds were almost immediately promised by some European countries and others hoped to follow suit. The programme was further expanded by a third international meeting at Amsterdam in November 1967.

The whole scheme was already a success. In 1967 twenty-one fellowships from the U.K. to other European countries were awarded, and eleven fellowships into the U.K. In 1968 the respective figures were fifty-seven and forty-five. During 1967–8 upwards of 109 study visits—usually for one or two weeks, with a rare maximum of six months—were supported outwards from the U.K. and twenty-six into the U.K. For specialized research conferences (limited to 25–100 participants) support was given from the funds held by the Royal Society for eleven in the same two years, and it is noted that in some instances the meetings have led to the establishment of continuing discussion groups. Stemming in no small measure from an interested and determined Foreign Secretary, the successful leadership of the Royal Society was not in doubt.

But there still remained the recurrent question as to the position of the humanities in all this growing interchange. However dominant the scientific elements—however relevant in some special measure the encouragement of international visitation in the fields of pure and applied science—there was surely a place somewhere for equivalent facilities in the field of the humanities. As has been noted above, our Continental colleagues were not indifferent to this need, and the Royal Society was well aware of it, to the point of embarrassment. The visit of the two Secretaries of the Royal Society to the Academy in February 1968 was followed by a hospitable Working Luncheon at the Royal Society's new apartments overlooking St. James's Park (surely the loveliest of back-curtains) on 12 June. Professor (Lord) Blackett presided as President of the Royal Society, and the Academy was represented by its President (Sir Kenneth Wheare), Lord Robbins, Dame Helen Gardner, Mr. J. W. Pope-Hennessy, and the Secretary. With Professor Blackett for the Royal Society were Lord

Fleck, Sir Harold Thompson, Professor M. J. Lighthill, Dr. D. C. Martin, and Dr. R. W. J. Keay.

The occasion might without undue exaggeration be described as something of a landmark. Beforehand, Professor Blackett had suggested in a letter to the Academy's Secretary that the following topics might be included in discussion:

(i) European exchanges.

(ii) Joint Activities, e.g. discussion meetings on scientific methods in archaeology and on other subjects; the question of technical terms about which Professor Kurti wrote to you some time ago.

(iii) Exchange of views on financing research in subjects borderline to both arts and science.

From the subsequent lunchtime discussion, which was sympathetic and helpful, the following main points arose:

(i) It was agreed that the Academy should consider the drafting of a scheme, comparable in principle with that which had been formulated by the Royal Society, for the development of scholarly interchange between selected foreign countries and the U.K. in both directions. The Royal Society's scheme, outlined above, was explained.

(ii) Both bodies would consider the formation of a joint committee for the purpose of reviewing scientific aids as used at present by the humanities (e.g. archaeology). How are these aids working out in practice? What questions arise in regard to their validity? In what direction is technical improvement desirable? In this connection the Academy's Secretary drew attention to the forthcoming twentieth anniversary of Willard Libby's exposition of his radiocarbon dating, probably the most important scientific contribution to the study of man since the days of the early stratigraphical geologists. Would not this anniversary provide a context for a joint review of this method in the light of its first and widespread experimental usage?

(iii) The Academy might wish to consider the formation of a joint committee with the Royal Society for the purpose of considering the formulation of terms for international usage.

From these proposals advance can be registered at the end of 1968 in two main directions. Towards the inauguration of an exchange programme on the precedent of the Royal Society, the first step was to collect a fund from non-Government sources as an encouragement to Government action when the Academy's next triennial budget should be presented to the Department of Education and Science in 1971. Accordingly, in first instance

(November 1968) the Academy's Secretary approached his old and influential friend, Lord Evans of Hungershall, in the hope that he might be moved to consult the Wates Foundation, which had already helped the Royal Society in similar circumstances. This he did, with welcome success. In May 1969 the Foundation generously placed a grant of £10,000 at the disposal of the Academy, with the added note that, should the scheme prove successful, the Founders might consider in the future a further grant of funds if, in the meanwhile, these had not been obtained from Government. To advise the Academy's Council on the administration of this and other relevant funds, an Overseas Policy Committee was set up under the chairmanship of the Academy's Foreign Secretary, Professor A. G. Dickens, Director of the Institute of Historical Research in the University of London.

Almost at the same time an unsolicited and generous grant was offered by the Leverhulme Trustees for the purpose of establishing a number of British Academy/Leverhulme Visiting Professorships on lines similar to those already established by the Trust in co-operation with the Royal Society. The benefaction is of £40,000 spread over five years, and is expected to provide for some four Visiting Professorships a year, each Professorship to last for three to four months, to enable the holder to lecture and carry out research in a selected university or other institution overseas. This and other developments lie outside the scope of the present review and details are therefore irrelevant; but the simultaneous action of the two Foundations constituted a good augury for the early establishment of a systematic policy of international collaboration in the field of the humanities.

Alongside these important administrative moves, the new spirit of co-operation between the Royal Society and the Academy found expression in the accepted proposal that the twentieth anniversary of radiocarbon dating should be marked by a jointly organized international symposium on 'The Impact of the Natural Sciences on Archaeology'; and a small committee was set up by Lord Blackett to work out details. (The Committee consisted of Dr. T. E. Allibone, F.R.S., who acted as chairman and secretary, Dr. I. E. S. Edwards, F.B.A., Keeper of Egyptian Antiquities at the British Museum, Dr. E. T. Hall, Director of the Research Laboratory for Archaeology and the History of Art in the University of Oxford, Dr. A. E. Werner, Keeper of the British Museum's Laboratories, and myself.) The symposium, the first occasion upon which the Royal Society and the British Academy had met together, was held at the Royal Society on the 11 and

12 of December 1969, with Professor Willard Libby, of the University of California, Los Angeles, as the principal guest, and was widely attended. Eighteen papers were read, primarily upon results and problems emerging from two decades of experience in the use of the radiocarbon method but extending to archaeomagnetism, archaeometry, thermoluminescence, magnetic methods of archaeological prospecting, pottery analysis, and a mathematical approach to seriation. Those who took part included, besides Professor Libby, Dr. Edwards, Mr. H. Barker and Dr. Werner of the British Museum, Dr. H. W. Catling of the Ashmolean Museum, Mr. E. T. Hall and Dr. M. J. Aitken of Oxford, Professor D. G. Kendall, F.R.S., and Professor H. Godwin, F.R.S., of Cambridge, Professor A. Sachs of Brown University, U.S.A., Professor B. Bannister of Arizona, Professor R. Berger, Dr. V. Buche, and Professor H. Suess of California, Dr. R. E. Linington of Rome, Dr. I. Scollar of Bonn, Dr. R. H. Brill of Corning, U.S.A., and Dr. A. A. Gordus of Michigan. The symposium was a success, and it may be hoped that further joint meetings of the kind may be held when occasion arises. During the symposium the Royal Society's Club, by invitation of the British Academy, felicitously entertained to dinner the contributing guests in the British Academy's apartments at Burlington House, formerly the home of the Royal Society. All this is as it should be and bodes well.

XIV

FROM PRESIDENT TO PRESIDENT

I AM well aware that what has just been written here above is an atrocious pun, and that poor Tennyson is turning in his grave. And I am going to make it worse by repetition. During the two decades of this chronicle it may fairly be affirmed that the British Academy has slowly but steadily broadened down from President to President. In 1949 it was still essentially an Edwardian survival. Better put, perhaps, it was an honourable coterie of estimable scholars of advancing age and proved attainment, a very senior Common Room with the windows closed upon an unquestioned or inadequately questioned environment. Appropriately, the world outside was physically invisible from its mahogany-panelled Council Room. Its annual Government grant was, expressively enough, a static £2,500. In 1969 that same Academy is a hard-working institution with fifteen active research-committees and aggregate research funds which support and encourage over a hundred beneficiaries (many of them under forty years of age). Its Government grant is in the neighbourhood of £300,000, and is rising responsively and confidently in the face of new needs. Incidentally, it has emerged from the dark recesses of Burlington Gardens into such daylight as penetrates to the august courtyard of Burlington House. There it is proud to follow literally in the footsteps of its elder colleague, the Royal Society, now promoted to the airy purlieus of St. James's Park. It is at last housed in the enclave of the Learned Societies *par excellence*, and its Fellows are no longer condemned to creep in through files of attendant examinees.

So then in the course of a couple of decades the Academy may be claimed to have broadened its scope and its efficiency beyond recognition. But, in saying that, I have no wish to be misunderstood. If it so happens that these decades have coincided with the tenure of some one particular Secretary, it would be regrettable should that circumstance be allowed to obscure the inner facts. Inevitably the Secretary has been the backbone and cerebral nerve of the skeleton; that indeed is his job. But the ribs and the meat on the bones and the mind at the top of them are not his, or his alone. It is at least just and proper that in this last chapter some slight attempt should be made to indicate the fashion in which during these formative years the Academy as a vital organism has really functioned; a phenomenon not wholly deducible from lists of committees and aggrading resources, however gratifying these be as a register of growing stamina.

Foremost in this summary recollection stands that formidable line of Presidents with which the Academy has been blest—nay, has blest itself—since 1950. (I go no further back since in the few months of my overlap with Harold Idris Bell I established no significant contact with that eminent papyrologist.) On other pages something has been said of the basic achievements of Sir Charles Webster as the Academy's President from 1950 to 1954. About this time he retired from his Chair and was hard at work, in some tiny hideout in Whitehall, on the official history of Bomber Command. This somewhat unlikely task and the overseas journeyings it involved, combined with expeditions to the Union Académique Internationale at Brussels and elsewhere, sustained some of the international interests with which he had identified himself in one way or another since the foundation of the League of Nations, which he had witnessed long ago at Versailles. And now for an hour or two each day he would focus his experienced mind upon the no less complex affairs of the British Academy, and he and I, as has been related, pooled and discussed ideas and counter-ideas with persistence and enthusiasm at the Athenaeum or at his hospitable flat at Swiss Cottage, and in the process became the closest of friends. Looking back, it is not difficult to see that the delicate (by no means easy) reshaping of the Academy's structure in those years, which was in a great degree Webster's work, was the prerequisite of all that was to follow. When David Knowles, with his unfailing generosity, wrote to me at the time of my retirement from the Academy's Secretaryship at the end of 1968, he allowed his kindliness to reverse the priorities but with that amendment he was right: 'I always regard you—along with Webster—as the Second Founder of the Academy, and you have borne the burden and heat of the day over the years when Webster could not do so.' Yes, Webster was veritably the Second Founder, and the four years when we worked together were those of a happy, sometimes happily disputatious, partnership in which it would never have occurred to either of us to discriminate personal values.

In the fullness of time it fell to us, Webster and the Secretary, to consider the problem of a successor-President. Gradually our thinking focused upon the Provost of Oriel. To him there were

7. Entrance to the British Academy's quarters in Burlington House since November 1968. These quarters, shared with the Chemical Society, were built in and about 1870 to the designs of R. R. Banks and Sir Charles Barry, and were occupied by the Royal Society until 1967.

8. Lord Robbins (President 1962–1967) receiving the 'Thank-offering to Britain Fund' from Mr. W. Behr (centre) and Sir Hans Kreb, F.R.S. (right).

two possible and equally fantastic objections: we had already had a Provost of Oriel as our President, and was it fit and decent that the present Provost, who happened to be a distinguished historian, should follow another historian in the Presidential Chair? We at least had no doubt in the matter, and when in due course our fireside proposal was put to the Council, this at once settled the matter by regarding both objections as positive qualifications. Sir George Clark proceeded to rule the Academy with undemonstrative but unqualified success from 1954 to 1958.

It was not long before my rapport with George Clark was second only to that with Charles Webster. We sipped our claret and settled the world and found life on the whole a pleasant place. We entertained and were entertained by Maccabaeans and others, and in a number of ways added to the interests and concerns of the Academy. Above all, in Clark's time was initiated that phase of intensive planning which was to mark one of the cardinal episodes in the Academy's history: the inauguration of the Rockefeller Inquiry into the present state of the provision for Humanistic research in Great Britain, accompanied by a comparative assessment of its more pressing needs. The Pilgrim Trust, with far-sighted wisdom, had already financed a pilot-scheme which had simultaneously emphasized some of these needs and indicated lines of advance. Now the Rockefeller Foundation, through the Academy, set out to systematize the whole problem, in consultation with Clark and initially under his chairmanship. It was a memorable moment and lent an unsurpassed distinction to the concluding months of Sir George Clark's Presidency.

Again, a little huddle of consultation between President and Secretary, with Charles Webster to make a trio. The time was approaching for a new President, and choice was not far to seek. Sir Maurice Bowra, who was to preside over the Academy's affairs from 1958 to 1962, is one of the most remarkable scholars whom it has been my pleasure to know. And before long we knew each other well. He descended upon Burlington Gardens in true Olympian character, thunderbolt and all. In more human terms he was (and is) one who can *laugh and shake in Rabelais' easy chair, Or in the graver gown instruct mankind.* Above all, he is the perfect travelling companion; and he and I have travelled a good many thousand miles together, talking and talking and occasionally perhaps listening. In our more idle moments we used to cruise in the Aegean, often with a crowd of acolytes with whom we would share our knowledge and our ignorance with equal zest; Maurice with an ebullience which became legendary and incidentally attracted to our companionship a number of our fellow-Academicians, who, be it said, lost nothing by occasional sophistry in the market-place. Within the more sober enclave of the Academy itself, Maurice's Presidency was distinguished in particular by two episodes. On the eve of his accession I had been responsible, working largely as a lone hand, for the creation of a British Institute of History and Archaeology in East Africa. Now, in 1961, he and I joined forces in the foundation of an Institute of Persian Studies in Teheran. It was a splendidly successful combined operation, sufficiently recounted in a previous chapter.

Maurice Bowra's second triumph, in his last year of office, was the completion and fruition of the Rockefeller Inquiry which had been handed over to him in its early stages by his predecessor. The story of this great scheme and of its consummation within a few hours of Bowra's last Presidential Address has likewise been told above. The day of that Address, 11 July 1962, marked a turning-point in the fortunes of the Academy as a patron of research. In our domestic saints' calendar it is worthy of commemoration as Clark–Bowra Day.

We have now reached a point at which our plain narrative might happily be interrupted by one of Arthur Bliss's majestic fanfares: heralding that giant polymath who was to govern the scene for the unusually extended period of five years, 1962 to 1967. Lionel Robbins, Lord Robbins, conducted the Academy's affairs, not merely with zest and understanding, but with an added quality which I can only attempt to describe in terms of sensibility and affection. Though the busiest of men—as a teacher of economics, as an administrator of our leading financial journal, as Chancellor of a university (almost chancellor of all universities), as an executive patron of the Opera, as a trustee and enthusiastic *habitué* of the National Gallery, and what else—he always had time to share his wisdom in seemingly effortless fashion at any level. During his long Presidency of the Academy he was in touch with every relevant activity; nevertheless, at our frequent working-lunches together at the Club our talk would take the Academy easily in its stride and would range beyond it into all manner of problems in all manner of places. They were light-hearted affairs, those lunches, to me full of stimulus and new knowledge, or old knowledge re-dressed. We began to know and value each other's prejudices (such as my very explicit dislike of those fluffy Renoir girls which at the time were so dear to the heart of the National Gallery), and surely sensitive prejudice is the ammunition of any good and lively conversation! They were happy days.

In these pages Lionel Robbins has already appeared as the recipient of the 'Thank-offering to Britain' Fund, with its touching and heartening over-tones. In the utilization of that great benefaction he took a deep and knowledgeable interest, and himself consented to give the first annual lecture under the benefaction. His subject was *Of Academic Freedom*, a cause for which he would no doubt go to the stake were the House of Lords not a more articulate medium of expression. Perhaps his outstanding contribution (amongst many others) to the Academy's growth has been his leadership in the organization of research, under the somewhat happier financial conditions which are beginning—just beginning—to prevail. Above all (and he must forgive this) the quiet wisdom and acute understanding with which he presided over the Academy's Council and proliferating committees will long remain a treasured memory of his fellow-Academicians in the full range of disciplines. The prolongation of his tenure of the Presidency beyond the normal four years has been matched only twice in the history of the Academy: once in wartime, and once in those strangely inactive early days, when Lord Balfour lent the majesty of his name for no less than seven years without imperilling it by the utterance of an annual address.

This brings me to the distinguished President who took his chair in 1967 and still (1969) happily presides alternatively from it or at longer range from that sweet City with her dreaming spires. Of Sir Kenneth Wheare it is not for me to speak save to recall the pleasure with which those of us who were closely concerned with his nomination heard of his modestly hesitant acceptance, and now delightedly observe as spectators his wise and humane fulfilment of his not inconsiderable trust.

This chapter is mainly a cavalcade of Presidents, but again it is perhaps desirable to avoid misconstruction. If there has been a tendency in a rapidly changing milieu for President and Secretary to constitute a sort of inner cabinet for primary discussion and often for personal approaches of an exploratory nature, it would be quite wrong to infer that the Academy has been governed by a tiny caucus: save in so far as efficient democracy necessarily subsumes efficient and concentrated leadership. In any case, to the two officers whom I have mentioned must at once be added the Treasurer who, in the person of Sir Roy Allen, has for many years administered the Academy's increasing and increasingly complex finances, with yeoman aid in detail from Miss D. W.

Pearson. But beyond this vital nucleus range the growing ranks of Fellows, who can now (since 1965) spread to a maximum of three hundred (without inclusion of the Senior Fellows) and, as scholars carefully selected for their individual prowess, may be relied upon to exercise a proper restraint upon autocracy!

In this last paragraph I have referred to the importance of limited 'primary discussion' and 'personal approaches' in the furtherance of the Academy's interests, and those phrases perhaps deserve a little amplification in the light of experience. Let it be affirmed with all emphasis that the Academy is *not* a sort of detached fragment of the university world. To begin with, it is in no way concerned, unless in an occasional research-project, with *education*. In the widest sense it assumes education but it is not professionally interested in the processes or trappings of education. Within my experience, at least three Fellows of the Academy have never been to a university at all. True, the Academy has since 1966 received its Government funds not, as previously, from H.M. Treasury direct but through the intermediation of the Department of Education and Science. So too has the Royal Society. This is largely a question of semantics and Parliamentary convenience. The D.E. & S. is full of understanding in these matters and the intervention of a State Department with the word 'Education' in its name has involved no significant change in the Academy's character or its established relations with Whitehall. Least of all is the Academy in any sense a sawn-off branch of the Civil Service, with whom nevertheless it has the friendliest interchanges. It is, *sui generis*; highly personal, and concerned at all levels rather with individual consultation than with more formal documentation.

Lastly, since this is a Secretary's personal record, a final word may be permitted about the Secretaryship itself. This chronicle began with the accumulative stranglehold of old age upon the advancement of the Academy some twenty years ago. It has told something of the successful efforts then made to mitigate this embarrassment. Paradoxically the present history is the handiwork of one who was recently Secretary in his latter seventies. What has happened to the vaunted policy of age-restraint? Happily that Secretary was the last of his kind. He was a throw-back to the era when all officers of learned societies, even secretaries, were expected to be honorary, part-time and, often enough in elderly retirement. In the interim for good or ill—but mostly for good— the world has changed, and the Academy with it. Even in 1949 the Secretaryship was in fact if not in name a whole-time task; on

Oxford Mail and Oxford Times photograph

9. Sir Kenneth Wheare (President 1967–) in action as Vice-Chancellor of Oxford University, November 1965.

The Times photograph

10. Dr. L. S. B. Leakey, F.B.A., at Burlington Gardens with the Secretary of the Academy (right), 1967.

accession the new Secretary quickly discovered that the Academy's cares were rarely absent from his mind. So much for part-time. As for recompense (save for a tiny expense-account which I think was at first £300), that was beyond all consideration. And so it remained for twenty years. Now and then the possibility of some sort of financial acknowledgement for what had indeed become a pretty full life was mooted by a kindly President. The Secretary's reply was adamant. It was in effect the Secretarial equivalent of the Empress Eugénie's alleged retort when her future royal husband made some sort of suggestion to her before he had been persuaded to offer marriage: 'Seigneur, ou Impératrice ou rien'. So the Secretary: for the dignity and efficiency of the Academy, to a Secretaryship of fully acknowledged status equivalent to that of a university professorship there was no viable alternative. And for that burden the finances of the Academy were not yet in adequate shape. The only answer, however deplorable, was to continue to tolerate the ageing Secretary until the Academy's income should reach a magnitude sufficient to justify, and be seen to justify, a Secretaryship of professorial grade. In consultation with D.E. & S. it was agreed that that happy situation was at last arising in 1968.

By the grace of providence the moment synchronized with the availability of an old friend, a Fellow of the Academy and an Under-Secretary in the Board of Trade. Happily, in Whitehall those whom the gods love retire young, and Mr. Derek Allen, of high repute as a numismatist and experienced in the administration of busy bureaux, was available and willing to shoulder the central burden of the Academy at an agreeable age. With good heart I wish him the pleasure that is labour too.

INDEX

158 INDEX